Through Others' Eyes

Also by Jeffrey C. Benton

A Sense of Place: Montgomery's Architectural Heritage, 1821–1951

The Very Worst Road: Travellers' Accounts of Crossing Alabama's Old Creek Indian Territory, 1820–1847

They Served Here: Thirty-three Maxwell Men

Respectable and Disreputable: Leisure Time in Antebellum Montgomery

Through Others' Eyes

Published Accounts of Antebellum Montgomery, Alabama

COMPILED BY
JEFFREY C. BENTON

NEWSOUTH BOOKS
Montgomery

NewSouth Books
105 S. Court Street
Montgomery, AL 36104

Published in the United States by NewSouth Books, a division of NewSouth, Inc., Montgomery, Alabama.

All illustrations in the book were provided as digital images by the Alabama Department of Archives and History, Montgomery, Alabama.

Publisher's Cataloging-in-Publication data

Through others' eyes : published accounts of antebellum Montgomery, Alabama / compiled by Jeffrey C. Benton
p. cm.
Includes index.

978-1-60306-258-9 (paperback)
978-1-60306-259-6 (ebook)

1. Montgomery (Ala.)—History—19th century. I. Title.

2014949888

Design by Randall Williams
Printed in the United States of America
by Ebsco Media

To my daughters,

Caroline and Catherine

Contents

Editor's Note on the Text

Each passage in this volume is transcribed exactly from the original source indicated at the beginning of the chapter. Misspellings, spelling variants, as well as grammatical and typographical errors follow the original sources. Punctuation varied from author to author, but all used commas more frequently than standard usage today; usage of colons and semi-colons also varied from contemporary practice. With few exceptions, errors in fact are reprinted without editorial comments.

The copies of the originals used in this volume are held by the Library of Congress or by the Special Collections, Ralph Brown Draughon Library, Auburn University. Most of the travel books are available online and at large university libraries.

Preface

T*hrough Others' Eyes*, like its companion volume, *The Very Worst Road: Travellers' Accounts of Crossing Alabama's Old Creek Indian Territory, 1820–1848*, grew out of my research on leisure activities in antebellum Montgomery. In the mid-1990s, while I was compiling those accounts, I also began collecting published accounts of antebellum Montgomery itself.

It was not, however, until the summer of 2009 that I was inspired to follow through with the project begun more than a decade earlier. Both the scholars and schoolteachers participating in "Slavery in Alabama: Public Amnesia and Historical Memory," a continuing education course for teachers conducted by the Alabama Humanities Foundation and the Alabama Department of Archives and History, provided the inspiration by reminding me of the power of primary sources.

In rereading the collected accounts, I began to compare memories of my own travels (unlike the writers of the published accounts in this book, I did not keep notes). Although my travels have given me perspective and a measure with which to evaluate different places, including Montgomery, my adopted hometown, they have serious limitations. I certainly have a more realistic understanding of the nine states and four foreign countries in which I have lived than I do of all fifty states and the thirty-two countries that I have merely visited.

One whirlwind visit, however, stands out: five days in Romania in 1993. I knew little about Romania before being selected from the U.S. Air War College faculty to travel to Bucharest to speak on the role of national armed forces in a liberal democracy, something foreign to the students in the Romanian War College. Unlike our four war colleges, Romania's not only had senior officers of the Romanian armed services but also parliamentarians, government bureaucrats, and representatives of the media.

In addition to formal lecture hall and classroom experiences, I was dined and toured and had several hours to explore the city alone and on foot.

A significant part of what was once known as the Paris of the Balkans had been leveled by Nicolae Ceausescu in a mad failed attempt to rebuild the city on a monumental scale; Napoleon, Hitler, and Stalin came to mind as I walked. Thanks to our military mission, I was also able to spend one day in Transylvania with a University of Texas professor. We visited a fortified Saxon (German) village that had no electricity, running water, or gas. Most shocking was looking in the home of a Gypsy family who had been slaves until the fall of Ceausescu in 1989, although slavery had been legally ended in Romania in 1918. I vividly remember looking into a room that had no furniture. Its only contents were a pile of rags on one side of the room for the females and another pile on the other side for the males—and in the middle, on the floor, a hunk of raw meat with several dogs licking up the blood. The point of this extended example is this: What do I really know about Romania, even with educated and knowledgeable people helping to interpret what I was seeing and experiencing—and what did most of those traveling through antebellum Montgomery really know about the city, its people, its values, and its manners?

In the "Prologue" that follows, I address how these limitations affected the accounts of antebellum visitors to Montgomery.

Acknowledgments

As MENTIONED ABOVE, I am indebted to the participants in the workshop on "Slavery in Alabama" organized by Alabama Humanities Foundation and the Alabama Department of Archives and History, especially to Mary Ann Neeley, who remembers more about Montgomery than others have ever heard, and Dr. Chaunda A. McDavis of Auburn University, who introduced me to James Redpath. My wife, Karen, has as usual undertaken the laborious task of proofreading the text; I want her to know that it is not a thankless task.

Through Others' Eyes

1

Prologue

Travel books were extremely popular in the nineteenth century. At least forty mention Montgomery, which, because of its location just off the Federal Road and near the head of navigation on the Alabama River, made it a natural transit point between the Seaboard States and the Gulf cities of Mobile and New Orleans.

Travel books, however, have their limitations, especially those by writers who only experienced cursory visits. Their comments tend to be mere sketches; they may capture a vague likeness of the place, but they rarely are portraits that capture the soul of the place. Consequently, the primitive state of roads, hotels, food, and the inhabitants themselves filled many inches of type. Some of those who wrote about antebellum Montgomery were famous, others were obscure; the length of the biographical comments that precedes each account indicates the authors' relative prominence. Of the twenty-seven writers included in this book, only Harriet Martineau and Fredrick Law Olmsted spent more than a few days in Montgomery and present content that exhibits depth of understanding. The entertainers Noah Ludlow, Sol Smith, and P. T. Barnum may have had extended visits or visited several times, but their accounts tend to be focused on themselves and to be rather frivolous. William Howard Russell managed to observe and analyze in a short time, but then he was a seasoned reporter for *The Times* of London and had access to everyone from Abraham Lincoln to Jefferson Davis. Others, such as Auguste Levasseur, an aide to the Marquis de Lafayette, and Francis Pulszky, who served Louis Kossuth in a similar capacity, were on semi-official visits and would, therefore, have been insulated to a degree from an ordinary experience. James Redpath, operating at the other extreme, traveled incognito so as to be able to interview thousands of slaves.

American chattel slavery was of great interest to the Europeans and to a somewhat lesser degree to the Northerners. As the century wore on, fewer Europeans would have remembered slavery in Europe; between 1787 and 1808, French and British slavery had been abolished, first domestically, then in their empires, and finally the legal slave trade itself. Slavery began to die out in the Northern States after the American Revolution—it was deemed incompatible with revolutionary ideals—and was essentially nonexistent in the Northern states as far as Northerners were concerned. So slavery had become, in the Southern phrase, the "peculiar institution."

Travelers to Montgomery saw slavery variously; many reveal their astonishment with the complexity of the system that they had previously understood so simplistically. Today, scholarship tends to discount or at least question what both Southern whites and blacks said about slavery at the time. Scholars think that many whites were delusional, or saw what they wanted to see, thought what they wanted to think, or knowingly warped reality. Scholars think that the slaves themselves, for obvious reasons, told whites what the slaves assumed or knew the whites wanted to hear. Furthermore, what travelers reported is more likely to have been hearsay conveyed by Southern whites or the travelers' own observations tempered by interpretations offered by Southern whites. Nevertheless, travelers' accounts do reveal a system that was diverse and complicated.

Views on Alabamians also varied: ignorant, crude, ill-mannered, superficially genteel, and materialistic at one extreme to seductive in their affability at the other, with ready familiarity and disarming hospitality. Because travelers were most often confined with Alabamians when in a stagecoach or on a steamboat, I have included accounts of both stage and river travel to and from Mobile. However, Alexander Mackay, writing in the 1840s, warns his readers of the danger of basing opinions on the "floating population" of the steamboats, stagecoaches, railways, and taverns. With a few exceptions, I have not included travel to the east of Montgomery. That is covered in this book's companion volume, *The Very Worst Road.*

There are two accounts that I would like to have included, but have not because they were only published well after the antebellum period. Although Alexis de Tocqueville's *Democracy in America*, which some think is the best analysis of the American nation, was published in 1835, his *Journey to America*, the compilation of notebooks that he kept during his 1831–32 trip, was not published until the twentieth century. In the latter, de Tocqueville recounts his two-day conversation with a young Montgomery lawyer in January 1832. The lawyer revealed the city's and Old Southwest's lawlessness, violence, and political and judicial corruption. The other account is a personal letter from John James Audubon to John Bachman of Mobile that has been published in *Selected Journals and Other Writings*, 1997. In his February 1837 letter, Audubon gives an account of witnessing Creek Indians being rounded up to be moved to Indian Territory (Oklahoma). Mary Boykin Chesnut's comments are so well known, they need not be reprinted in this book.

Although this book is nominally about travelers' views of antebellum Montgomery, I have not only included travel to and from Montgomery, as explained in the previous paragraph, but I have also included accounts of excursions into Montgomery's hinterland. These, too, provide significant information about the people, the land itself, and the planters' cotton market economy, although the subsistence economy of yeoman farmers or plain people is entirely missing.

The study of natural history had been a fashionable pastime for gentlemen, and even some ladies, during the Enlightenment of the eighteenth century. By the nineteenth century, it had become more of a specialized interest; in fact, the word "scientist" came into use in the 1830s. These travelers' accounts reveal a continuation of the fashionable pastime and the general knowledge of natural history of people of education, as well as specialized knowledge of scientists. The emphasis is on geology and flora. Fauna is lacking—although several alligators, a horny toad, and birds are mentioned.

Contrary to the values of the formally educated Europeans, Americans in general and Alabamians in particular are seen as driven by materialism, to the neglect of spiritual and intellectual values. After all, it was Alabama Fever, the prospect of getting rich quickly with cotton, that attracted Americans from the relatively more civilized Seaboard States to the Old Southwest. Perhaps the travelers should not have been so harsh, and not all of them were. At the end of the antebellum period, Montgomery was just over forty years old, although some remarked that those forty years were but little marked by progress.

A comparison of the time lapse between when the visits were made and when many of the books were published reveals that most of these books were like today's media. There was little time before publication to read, mark, study, and inwardly digest—to observe, question, and analyze. Although they did not conform to a 24-hour news cycle, many of these travelers were similar to today's "talking heads" and instant experts. That said, these accounts offer a captivating insight into the antebellum Montgomery that no scholarly work with its studied objectivity and scholarly disinterest can offer. Just because these accounts are so personal, just because their authors are real flesh and blood people with such prejudices—who could top Mrs. Royall—we can vicariously travel with them to antebellum Montgomery.

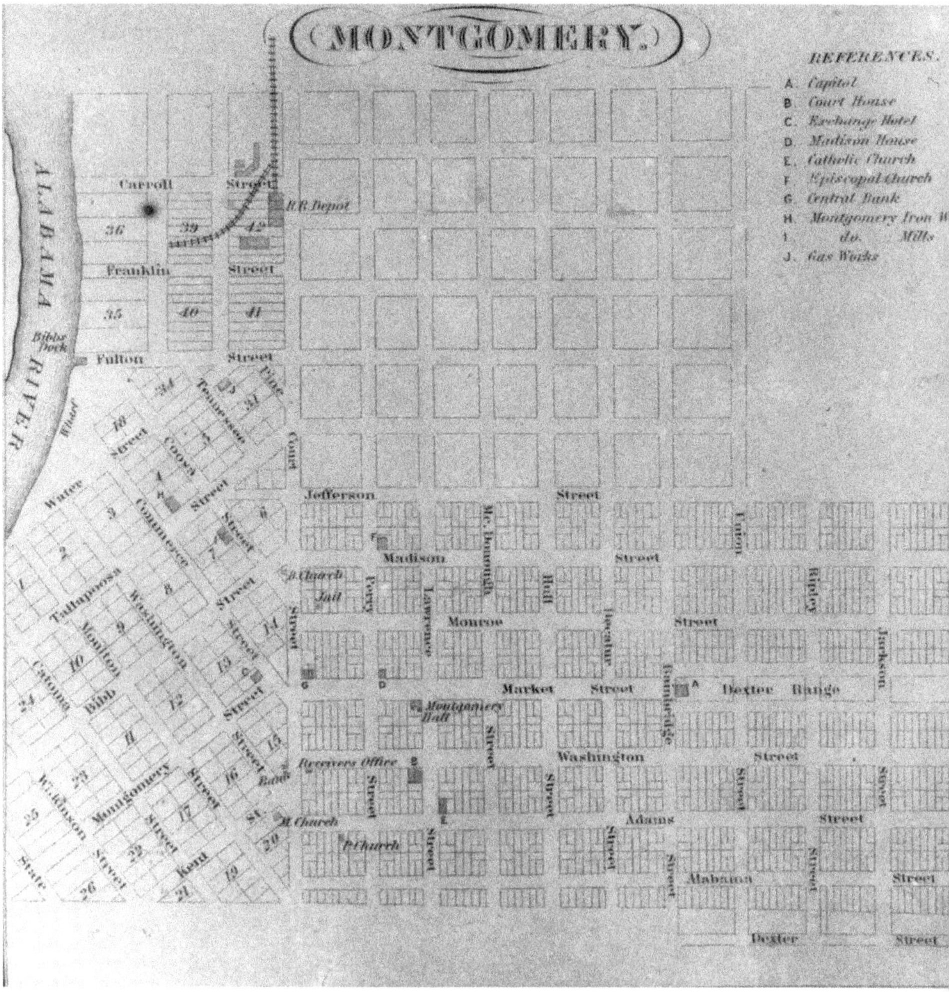

Plan of the City of Montgomery, 1852. The north-south grid followed that laid out for New Philadelphia, and the diagonal grid that for East Alabama.

Later photograph of 1821 Freeny's Tavern/Montgomery Tavern/Bell Tavern, Montgomery's first brick building. This building was the site of the grand ball held for the Marquis de Lafayette on 4 April 1825.

2

Auguste Levasseur

April 1825

Auguste Levasseur was the personal secretary of the Marquis de Lafayette and the chronicler of Lafayette's triumphant 1824–25 tour of the United States. In addition to Levasseur, the marquis's son, George Washington Lafayette, and his valet, Bartien, accompanied Lafayette, the last living major general of the American Revolution and a great national hero as the United States approached its fiftieth anniversary. Levasseur was an astute observer of the American scene; his account is realistic. Both he and Lafayette are more interested in the Creek Indians they visited immediately before being feted in Montgomery than they are in the elite of Alabama. In fact, they brought one Creek with them to Montgomery, Chillie, the eldest son of the assassinated Creek chief, William McIntosh. Levasseur served Lafayette for three years after returning to France and did not publish the journal until 1829.

Auguste Levasseur, *Lafayette in America in 1824 and 1825; or Journal of a Voyage to the United States*, 3 vols. Trans. John Davidson Godman (Philadelphia: Carey and Lea, 1829), II: 83–85.

We quitted Line Creek on the 3d of April, and the same day General Lafayette was received at Montgomery, by the inhabitants of that village, and by the governor of the state of Alabama, who had come from Cahawba with all his staff and a large concourse of citizens, who had assembled from great distances to accompany him. We passed the next day at Montgomery, and left it on the night of the 4th and 5th, after a ball, at which we had the pleasure of seeing Chilli M'Intosh dance with several beautiful women, who certainly had little idea that they were dancing with a savage. The parting of M'Intosh with the general was a melancholy one. He appeared overwhelmed with sinister presentiments. After having quitted the general and his son, he met me in the courtyard; he stopped, placed my right hand on his, and elevating his left hand towards heaven, "Farewell," said he, "always accompany our father and watch over him. I will pray to the Great Spirit also to watch over him, and give him a speedy and safe return to his children in France. His children are our brothers; he is our father. I hope that he will not forget us." His voice was affected, his countenance sad, and the rays of the moon falling obliquely on his dark visage, gave a solemnity to his farewell with which I was deeply moved. I wished to reply to him, but he quitted me precipitately and disappeared.

At two o'clock in the morning, we embarked on the Alabama, on board the steamboat Anderson, which had been richly and commodiously prepared for the general, and provided with a band of musicians sent from New Orleans. All the ladies of Montgomery accompanied us on board, where we took leave of them; and the moment the reports of the artillery announced our departure, immense fires were lighted on the shore. Our voyage as far as the Tombigbee was delicious. It is difficult to imagine any thing more romantic than the elevated, gravelly, and oftentimes wooded shores of the Alabama. During the three days we were on it, the echoes repeated the patriotic airs executed by our Louisiania musicians. We stopped one day at Cahawba, where the officers of government of the state of Alabama had, in concert with the citizens, prepared entertainments for General Lafayette, as remarkable for their elegance and good taste, as touching by their cordiality and the feelings of which they were the expression. Among the guests with whom we sat down to dinner, we found some countrymen whom political events had driven from France. They mentioned to us, that they had formed part of the colony at Champ D'Asile. They now lived in a small town they had founded in Alabama, to which they had given the name Gallopolis [today's Demopolis]. I should judge that they were not in a state of great prosperity. I believe their European prejudices, and their inexperience in commerce and agriculture, will prevent them from being formidable rivals of the Americans for a length of time.

Cahawba, the seat of government of Alabama, is a flourishing town, whose population, although as yet small, promises to increase rapidly, from its admirable situation at the confluence of the Cahawba and Alabama.

The state of Alabama, which, like Mississippi, was formerly part of Georgia, and with which its early history is intimately connected, received a territorial governor from congress in 1817, and was admitted into the federation as an independent state in 1816 [1819]. Its population, which in 1810 was only 10,000, had risen to 67,000 in 1817, and is at present 128,000. In this estimate of the population I do not include the Indian tribes of Choctaws, Cherokees, and Chickasaws, residing in the east and west of the state.

From Cahawba we descended the river to Claiborne, a small fort on the Alabama. The general was induced by the intreaties of the inhabitants to remain a few hours, which were passed in the midst of the most touching demonstrations of friendship. Mr. Dellet, who had been appointed by his fellow citizens to express their sentiments, acquitted himself with an eloquence we were astonished to meet in a spot, which, but a short time before, only resounded with the savage cry of the Indian hunter.

A little below Claiborne, I remarked that the banks of the Alabama were much lower; when we had passed the mouth of the Tombigbee, we found ourselves in the middle of low marshy meadows, but apparently very fertile. Finally, we arrived on the 7th of April, in Mobile bay, at the bottom of which is situated a city of the same name.

The distance we had traversed in three days, and which was more than three hundred miles, on account of the windings of the river, formerly required a month or six weeks in ascending, and half the time in descending. This shows what a prodigious revolution the application of steam to navigation will effect the commercial relations of a country.

The city of Mobile, which is the oldest establishment in the state . . .

3

Karl Bernhard, Duke of Saxe-Weimar-Eisenach

January 1826

Karl Bernhard, Duke of Saxe-Weimar-Eisenach (1792–1862), a German duke in the service of the king of the Netherlands, fought in three major campaigns against Napoleon. Bernhard continued in the service of the Dutch king, and rose to the rank of lieutenant general in 1831. The king facilitated the duke's 1825–26 journey to Canada and the United States. Bernhard visited Thomas Jefferson at Monticello and was, in fact, most comfortable in cities and with members of the American elite. Like most European visitors, he disliked slavery. His journal, which Bernhard initially intended not to publish, reveals the keen observation of detail and discernment of a mature, experienced, sophisticated man.

Bernhard, Duke of Saxe-Weimar-Eisenach, *Travels Through North America During the Years 1825 and 1826*, 2 vols. (Philadelphia: Carey, Lea, and Carey, 1828), II: 31–33.

We arrived at Montgomery about two o'clock. In the night it had frozen, but the day had solaced us with the warmth of spring.

Montgomery lies on the Alabama river, a navigable stream, which rises about two hundred and twenty miles above this place, and after it has joined itself to the Tombigbee, empties into the Mexican gulf, below Mobile. The town contains about one thousand two hundred inhabitants, of both complexions. It has two streets, which are very broad, tolerably good houses, one, not yet finished, of brick, which material is very bad here. This place was first laid out about five years ago, and has already a very lively appearance. On the bank of the river, they were employed in loading two steam-boats with cotton bales, as, within a few days, the river had risen five feet, and the navigation was once more carried on with animation.

The journey by water from Montgomery to Mobile, is four hundred miles, and as we intended to go this way, we took a look at the two steam-boats lying here, the Steubenville and Hornet, bound for Mobile. We chose the Steubenville, which gave out to start on the next day. The construction of both these boats, and their arrangement, is far inferior to that of the steam-boats in the north: every thing was coarser, and displayed the difference between the civilization of the two different sections of the union. This town is so new, that the original forest still stands between the houses. In a street there was a well digging; I discovered by this that the earth was exceedingly well adapted to brick-making, and that an industrious man, who should establish a kiln here, must make a handsome profit on the business. The bricks which they sell here at ten dollars a thousand, are scandalous. Of the inhabitants I heard nothing commendable: and how can this young town, whose situation, at least in summer, is unhealthy, have a fixed character; how can it attain a high degree of cultivation? All come here for the purpose of amassing property, or are driven here by the prostration of their fortunes, in their old residence!

CHAPTER XVII.

Journey from Montgomery, on the Alabama river, to Mobile, and residence in that city.

The Steubenville, commanded by Captain Grover, is of one hundred and seventy tons, and has a high pressure machine, of fifty horse-power. Machines like these are very dangerous, and therefore prohibited in the Netherlands. The machine of the Steubenville was made in Pittsburg. The body of the boat is occupied by the cargo, the cabins are upon deck. The dining-room has twelve births; behind this is a gallery with some apartments; the last one was hired by us. Before we sailed, two Indians came on board, who wondered very much at my double barrelled gun, with percussion locks; they had never seen such fire-arms before; I permitted them to discharge it, and gave them some of the copper caps, at which present they testified great delight.

We went down the river very swiftly, sixteen miles an hour. The banks of the river near Montgomery are rather high, they consist of red earth, with many spots of flint, and covered with willow-growth. We came only a distance of eighteen miles, to a place called Washington, where the Hornet lay, and where we also were stopped, to remain during the night for the purpose of taking in wood and cotton. On account of the number of sand banks, the navigation of the river must be dangerous; the captain assured me that the experienced pilot then on board, had one hundred dollars per month pay, so seldom are the officers of the boats here, accustomed to the localities!

The next morning we moved on at break of day, with considerable rapidity; but we soon stopped again, to take in some cotton bales, which lay ready in a wood on the shore. We had above four hundred bales already on board. The hold of the boat was full, the space between the machine and the first cabin was filled, as well as the space about the cabins, and the roof over them. There was no room left for exercise in walking, and in the cabin it was very dark. The first delay lasted about an hour; as soon as we were in motion again, we were obliged to stop for several hours, as one of the two pipes fell, and drew the other with it. The steward standing near, was wounded. We pursued our journey about midday, and laid by again towards sunset to take in wood, and remained for the night, as the water in the river had fallen, and the sand banks were numerous in this vicinity.

We went on shore to look about, and found ourselves near to a plantation with extensive cotton fields, a cotton gin, and a large cotton press. There is a vast quantity of cotton seed left, more than is required for the next year's planting, and the overplus is used for manure. I am well convinced, that with a small trouble and little expense, a very good oil could be expressed from this seed. It was thrown out in great heaps, which contained so much heat, that it was impossible to keep my hand in it a moment. The breadth of the river is here said to be three hundred yards, but I cannot believe it to be so much. The right bank may be about sixty feet high, it rests partly on sandstone, and consists of many layers of soil; the left bank is lower.

Both are grown up with wood, close to the water's edge with willows, and farther back with different sorts of trees; lofty oaks, live oaks, and white oaks, which only flourish in the south, with plane trees, hickories, and other nut-bearing trees, here and there with beech, ash, and alder, and also with tall green cane. If it were not so warm and unhealthy during the summer, a residence here would be delightful. We saw upon the river many flocks of wild geese and ducks, and upon the shore several buzzards. The river makes a number of turns, and contains several islands; yet the most of them are merely sand banks. Upon them lie fallen trees, of which passing vessels must take great care. On the banks were canoes, which, in the Indian fashion, were hewed out of a single tree.

On the 6th of January, the boat was under way before daybreak; she stopt at Cahawba till ten o'clock, to take in wood. This place has its name from a small river, which here flows into the Alabama. It lies upon the right hand bank of the river, here rather high. It was founded about five years ago, and it is already the capital of the state. With all this advantage, it contains only three hundred inhabitants of all sorts, and it is to be feared that its population will not increase, as the present legislature of Alabama, has resolved to change the seat of government to Tuscaloosa.

4

Noah Ludlow

January 1827

Noah Miller Ludlow (1795–1886), a native of New York City, began his actor-manager career in Kentucky in 1815. Later he managed theaters in New Orleans, St. Louis, and Mobile, as well as being the first actor to play in the more isolated towns of the Old Southwest. He partnered with Sol Smith from 1835 to 1853. Not only was he an excellent comedic actor himself, but he also presented outstanding actors to his audiences. *Dramatic Life As I Found It* chronicles his thirty-eight years as an actor and manager. The excerpted passage reveals something of the theater in early Montgomery. His theatrical offerings were dignified and respectable. Although he was a rather unhappy man, this excerpt reveals Ludlow's love of the absurd and appreciation of practical jokes—qualities almost exclusively confined to actors and entertainers in this book.

N. M. Ludlow, *Dramatic Life As I Found It* (St. Louis: G. I. Jones and Co., 1880), 298–303.

CHAPTER XXIX

...About the 10th of December we started for Montgomery, Alabama, then a small town of about fifteen hundred inhabitants, situated on the Alabama River, near the head of navigation. It has since become a city of considerable importance. I was induced to visit this town by a gentleman who assured me we would be well supported there in proportion to the limited population; but as he was landlord of the principal hotel, and had the only room large enough for us to perform in, I had some misgivings as to the beneficial result, knowing that a man's interest will sometimes warp his judgment. However, the Black Warrior River was not at that particular time in good boating condition, and there was no boat then at Tuscaloosa ready to depart for Mobile; therefore I concluded to go to Montgomery, where the chances of getting to Mobile, *via* the Alabama River, were more frequent, and at the same time ascertain what the town might be able to do in the way of theatricals, having an eye to a future and more lengthened season than I could now make in that town. To accomplish this journey to Montgomery we were obliged to hire land-conveyances, such as a heavy road-wagon with two horses, light wagons and saddle-horses. The journey, if I remember rightly, occupied three days, and was rather a rough one; yet not without some fun attached to it, in the minds of young and adventurous persons. As an instance of this kind I will relate an occurrence that took place on the evening of our second day's journey. We halted about sundown of this day at a residence on the roadside, consisting of two or three log-cabins, surrounded by cotton-fields, everything having the appearance of a well-to-do farming homestead. We asked if we could obtain "entertainment" there for the night,—meaning supper and beds for ourselves, and stabling and feed for our horses; to our question the reply was, we could. The owner of the house—who was the man we addressed—was a tall, huge-proportioned man, with a good-natured face; and his wife—whom we saw as we entered—was as tall in proportion, for a woman, as he was for a man. This tall pair were comfortably clad in home-made linsey-woolsey; and Ned Caldwell, who was always ready with some apt quotation, eyeing them from head to foot, whispered in my ear, "There were giants in those days." We observed here and there, dodging around, five or six children, and as many black ones of different sizes and ages, and all staring at the odd cavalcade entering the doors of the log cottages, quite as strange-looking to them as they were to us. An immediate onslaught was commenced upon the chickens, and negroes were dispatched to the barn and out-houses in search of eggs; in short, a general stir commenced at once to provide supper for a small army of hungry people. In the meantime there was a general washing and cleaning away of the dust of the road, preparatory to our evening meal. It was a tedious time ere supper was ready, but when it came it was abundant and substantial, consisting of sundry dishes of chicken fried in cream, eggs and ham at one end of the table and ham and eggs at the other,—no great variety, but all good; added to which were hot biscuit, fresh from the oven, delicious, sweet butter, and coffee that was a nosegay of most delicate flavor, especially to hungry people. All being seated at the table, the landlady took her position at a side-table and served out the coffee. As I was being seated, I discovered one of my company, Mr. "Ned" Caldwell, at the opposite end of the table, with his hair standing up like porcupine quills; his shirt-collar unbuttoned and spread back, and his eyes in "fine frenzy rolling," surveying the scene around him. On each side of and a little way behind him were two young negro boys, one about eight, the other about twelve years of age; behind my chair were, in like manner, two somewhat younger than the others. These four had each a *torch* of "light-wood," to speak the vernacular of that country, or as I would say, pitch-pine knots; and these being lighted, cast a wild and weird appearance upon the faces and objects around.

Perhaps I should explain here that the using of these torch-lights was in consequence of these people not having just then any candles at their command. Caldwell, who had taken two or three extra drinks of whiskey, of some he had brought with him, was just in the humor to imagine himself some great potentate, surrounded by his court, at a banquet. The first remark that he made was: "This likes me well! This is feasting in the Oriental, the Eastern style,—Tippoo Sahib with his retainers on a foraging excursion." At the same moment his eye rested on the largest negro boy, who stood near him, and who was clad in the most primitive kind of costume, namely, a cotton shirt scarcely long enough to be decent, over which was a coarse woollen jacket, and this was all. Caldwell surveyed him from head to foot, then said in a pompous, tragic manner, "Friend, what is thy name?" To which the negro replied, "Sip, massa" "Sip," repeated Caldwell, "meaning Scipio?" The darkey smiled and nodded, yes. "Surnamed Africanus?" The boy nodded again. "Scipio Africanus, stand further from the presence; [with his hand waving him back] for, to say the truth, I like not the contiguity nor the superfluity of the perfume of thy epidermis; it partakes not of the 'Sabeau odors from the spicy shores of Araby the blest;' [then drawing his chair nearer the table] nevertheless, [quoting from "King Lear"] 'I retain you as one of my hundred!' But I do not like the fashion of your garments; you will say they are Persian attire,—let them be changed!" During this harangue the company generally had paused and put on serious faces, in order to humor the joke. The landlord and his wife stared in wonderment, and the darkeys tried to smile, but looked frightened rather than amused. Supper was soon over, and all retired for the night to such accommodations as the family could afford them. These were rough, but clean; and, being tired, all slept soundly. I arranged overnight with our host to let us have breakfast by the time the sun rose the next day. At the time appointed it was ready, and so were we, and all sat down to a substantial breakfast, similar to the meal of the previous night. Before getting breakfast, Ned Caldwell had discovered that his horse was lame, or rather the horse he had hired at Tuscaloosa, and which was to be sent back with the return of the teamster of the baggage-wagon that I had hired. This discovery was annoying Caldwell very much, and he had been talking with our host about hiring a horse from him to perform the remainder of the journey, leaving his lame horse with him, to be exchanged on the return of the wagoner; and the fresh animal's hire was to be paid in advance. Noticing that I seemed to be the head of the party, the man came to me to ask what he had best do; saying he would be willing to let the gentleman have the horse, and had partly promised him he would, but that one of the friends of the gentleman (pointing to Sam Jones, one of my company, who was then walking at a short distance) had just then told him he must not regard what that man (meaning Caldwell) said, for he was a little *deranged;* and that he (Jones) was taking him on to the insane asylum at Philadelphia; that he had fallen in with this company on the road, and purposed to continue with them as far as Montgomery, after which he should proceed alone with him. I saw at once that there was some joke on foot among the young men, which they were playing off on Ned Caldwell. Our host was a kind-hearted man, and said: "I would let the poor gentleman have the horse, but his friend told me that I must positively refuse to let the horse go; that the lameness complained of was only temporary; that the horse would frequently limp after standing all night; but once on the road, in a little while the lameness would disappear, and he would get along as well as usual." While we were talking, Caldwell stepped up to get a final answer from our host, and I went to the stable to learn what was the real difficulty, should there be any at all. Jones, seeing me go towards the stable, followed; and when there I said, "Jones, what is the matter with Caldwell's horse?" He burst into a hearty laugh, and replied, "Nothing is the matter with him." "Well," I said, "what is the matter with Ned?" "O, nothing; it is only a joke we are playing off on him, to pay him for some of his own; you know he is addicted to practical joking. The fact is, while we were dressing this morning he said, 'I'll bet ten dollars my horse is lame, for I dreamed last night he was.' We all laughed at him." And Jones continued, "I went out quickly to the stable, and hunting round, found a thorn from a locust tree, which I stuck into one of the hind feet of his horse, but in such a way that I could easily pull it out again, leaving the horse without any real injury, but causing him to limp while it was there, as soon as he pressed his foot to the ground. I had not been out of the stable many minutes when Caldwell came to the house and said, 'Now, what do you think *of dreams?* I told you I should find my horse *lame,* and he is lame.'" Having heard Jones's explanation, I returned to the house, he having promised me he would immediately pull the thorn from the horse's foot. I found Caldwell fretting and fuming, and angrily censuring our host for making a promise to him and then breaking it; to which the other returned no reply, but walked away, looking at Ned pitifully, and pointing to his own forehead, nodded to me, as much as to say, "Poor fellow! mad as a March hare!" As I then understood the real state of the affair, I finally succeeded in persuading Caldwell to have his horse brought out, telling him it was probably only a little stiffness, that would be removed by exercise; to which he replied, he supposed there was no other way left for him, and as we had but one short day's journey then to make, if the horse continued lame he would get off his back and lead him the remainder of the journey. We were soon ready to start, and in the meantime I had talked with our landlord,—but saying nothing in regard to Caldwell,—giving him my name and telling him I was going to Montgomery to open a theatre there, and should he visit that town within the next two weeks he would probably find me at the principal hotel. He said he had some law business to attend to in Montgomery in a few days, and he thought we might meet again there. And so away we started, Ned on his supposed lame horse, that now hardly limped at all; our host standing in the door, looking at Ned and then at me, and pointing to his forehead, as though saying, "Poor fellow! mad! mad!"

We reached Montgomery about sundown of that day,—Caldwell's horse not in the least lame after the first half-mile of travel; but this lameness was a mystery to Caldwell until one night about a week after our opening at Montgomery, when, our evening's entertainment being over, three or four of the performers, with myself, were passing through the barroom of the hotel, when suddenly I came in contact with my tall host of the road, who had come, as he had previously said he would. He seemed glad to see me, and said he had been present at the evening's performance, and had been very much amused. After a few minutes' conversation, he said: "What became of the crazy man that was travelling with you? Do you know, I saw a man that *showed* with you to-night who reminded me of him? I never saw two men more alike. I would be glad to see that man, just to ask him if he hasn't a crazy brother." "Well," I said, "you can do that; here he stands behind you." With this I called Caldwell to me, and said: "Here is our host with whom we stayed the night before we reached Montgomery." "Oh, yes," said Ned; "this is the man that first would, and then he wouldn't?" The tall man stared, and seemed dumbfounded, but at last said: "Why! you are not the crazy man, are you?" "Crazy? d—n no! what put that into your head?" Just then Jones, who was standing at my elbow, made a start to go away; but I caught him by the coat-tail, held him, and compelled him to reveal the whole hoax he had passed upon Ned. We all had a hearty laugh, and Jones only got off by paying for a game supper for the party of four.

The room that we performed in at Montgomery was, perhaps, the most inconvenient place that ever the descendants of Thespis had to encounter. It was in the upper story of a very large, roughly built frame house, that was called a "hotel;" the garret, or topmost portion of which had been fitted up by some amateurs to perform plays in. The only way of reaching this attic temple of the muses, for either actors or audience, was by a flight of rough stairs on the *outside* of the building, and these seemed almost interminable; then, when you had reached the top of them, you had to make your entrance through a *window,* so low that a person of ordinary height had to stoop to get into the room. This room was fitted up with rough seats without any covering, and all on a dead level. There were no dressing-rooms contiguous to the stage; therefore the performers were compelled to dress in their own rooms of the stories below, and, wrapped in cloaks, thread their way among the audience to the stage. If a change of dress was required during the progress of a play, it had to be done behind a temporary screen across one corner of the room, and behind the back scene. I was told the room had been fitted up for some amateur actors of the town; of these the principal ones were a Mr. G——, a lawyer, and two schoolmasters, a Mr. V—s and a Mr. B—k. The first-named gentleman afterwards became a judge, and subsequently to that a United States senator. I believe all three are now dead.

Our season consisted of only two weeks, for the town did not pay; and those two weeks were the *first performances* by a *regular dramatic company in Montgomery.* I am told that town has now a very well arranged theatre, a largely increased population, and in years not long past, supported the Drama very well.

5

James Stuart

March 1830

James Stuart (1775–1849) successfully participated in Scottish Whig political affairs as a lawyer, justice of the peace, officer in the Fifeshire yeomanry, and functionary in several minor posts. Stuart was involved in a number of altercations in the press, in court, and in the street. He killed Sir Alexander Boswell in a duel; although tried, he was acquitted. Nevertheless, his political career suffered. Consequently, Stuart toured the United States for three years, and subsequently published his accounts to popular acclaim. His accounts, however, are as much from his reading as from his personal observation. Although he is positive towards the United States, he is critical of slavery and concludes that the hardships of travel in the South render the experience not worth the effort.

James Stuart, *Three Years in North America*, 3 vols. (Edinburgh: Robert Cadell, 1833), II: 203–209.

We reached Montgomery, the capital of Alabama,* in the evening; but the circuit being here, it was very difficult to find accommodations at either of the hotels. The landlord of the hotel where we stopped smiled, when I asked if I could have a separate bed-room. As soon, therefore, as I had my portmanteau deposited in a place of security, I sallied forth, under the guidance of one of the waiters, with a view to find out a lodging. I was told that Major Johnson, a Scottish gentleman, who is well known

* Stuart was incorrect. At the time of his visit in 1830, Tuscaloosa was the state's capital. It had moved from Cahaba in 1826, and would not be moved to Montgomery until 1845.

in the United States, on account of the exertions he made to save part of the Archives at Washington, on occasion of the British incursion, resided in the suburbs, and was always glad to see his countrymen. It turned out, unluckily, when I went to his house, that neither he nor any of his family were at home. I called at two or three other places which were pointed out to me, but had no better success, and returned to the hotel without attaining my object. The bar-keeper, however, after some talk, took pity on me, and told me he would put me in a double-bedded room, into which he should take care that no one should have right from him to enter; but that I must keep the door bolted, to prevent any one from coming into the room and taking possession, when he found only one of the beds occupied. I need not say that I obeyed orders; but I had not observed that there were two doors in the room to be secured, and only secured one. About the end of my first sleep, I was awoke by the noise of an intruder in the room. He brought no light with him. I started out of bed, and called, "Who's there?" He answered, "I'm, I'm Tomie Collins." Whoever you are, I replied, you must get out of the room,—both beds are taken. I hurried him out of the room without a moment's delay. I found the door at which he had entered, and had it bolted immediately. When I rose very early next morning, I discovered that the door of the hotel had not only not been locked, but had been standing open all night. I see in the newspapers, which I have got, published here, that boarding and lodging may be had by the year, in the best hotels in the neighbourhood, for 100 dollars.

On the following morning, I started by the stage for Mobile, on the Gulf of Mexico. There is steam-navigation from Montgomery to Mobile by the Alabama River; but the steam-vessels are more for the conveyance of cotton than of passengers; and the distance by the river, about 400 miles, is more than twice as long as by land. I had only one fellow-traveller in the stage, Captain Wade. He was acquainted with the country; but I believe he, as well as I, thought the driver had got us into a scrape, by preferring the ford to the bridge over the river, on our way to the south of Montgomery. We were all but swamped. The water got into the carriage; but the American drivers, thought very fond of sailing close by the wind, never run any hazard, as far as I have seen, without being sure that they will be able to extricate themselves. On the road near the river, we met an immense waggon load of whisky proceeding to Montgomery. The driver stopped and saluted; and the driver of the whisky allowed our driver to take as much of it from a great greybeard as he chose. He had also the courtesy to offer to the inside passengers as much of the liquor as we liked. But, while we acknowledged his kindness, neither of us had any disposition, so early in the morning, to hob and nob with him.

Not long after leaving the river, the stage passed through the first prairie land that I have seen, consisting of large undulating pastures, which never seem to have been covered with wood; on the skirts of which are fine forest trees, and frequently dropping trees, and clumps of wood adorning the plains.

Before I saw the prairie land, I was impressed with the notion that the prairies were great arid plains, almost entirely level; but the first prairie I now passed convinced me of my mistake, as it consisted of waving ground, necessarily of good soil, from the beautiful sward of grass rising from it. This is the character of a great part of the prairie land; but there are some entirely level plains in Louisiana. The great prairie land of America bears, as remarked by Darby, a close resemblance in geographical position, and in characteristic marks, to the Steppes of Asia. The inhabitants, too, of each of those districts have been free, as the plains over which they roam, knowing no luxury beyond the chace, nor any pursuit beyond their herds and their fields.

I can hardly trust myself to describe the prairie lands of this and the western states, where I afterwards was. The variety of their beauty is such, and their style and appearance altogether approaches so much to the English park, after it has been adorned at great cost, and with all the taste which generations of proprietors have possessed, that it is much safer for me to give the statements of Mr. Flint, who has seen more of the country than I have done, than to attempt to give any idea of their magnificence myself, under the very vivid impressions they have made on me of their extraordinary beauty. The name prairie is French, denoting a meadow.

"The first view of a prairie will probably excite more surprise in the mind of a traveller in the United States than the grandest objects of nature. Riding day after day through forests, in which the cleared land is not of sufficient extent to interrupt the general aspect of wood, he breaks at once upon the view of a fine open country,—he beholds extensive plains of the most soft and beautiful verdure, covered with flowers of every scent and hue. Occasionally on the prairie, and often in their centre, are clumps of fine trees, especially of the oak and black walnut, so charmingly disposed, that the traveller can hardly believe that they have not been placed by the hand of man. The views of tracts of country of this description are in many places far more extensive than are to be met with in any country, where land has been laid out in this way artificially, with a view to its beauty, and to increase its value to its possessor. The prospect from the high grounds that often surround the prairies, comprehending verdant lawns, large forests, through which vast rivers are rolling their mighty masses of water, and fine hills in the distance, with cottages, cattle, horses, and deer, is altogether as fine as can be conceived anywhere."

The grass of the prairies is tall and rather coarse, but in the early stages of its growth, it furnishes succulent and rich food for cattle; and if it was cut in that state, or a little afterwards, it would make excellent winter fodder; but as the summer advances, the grass becomes tough, and of course, when cut in that state, it does not become so nourishing food for the winter. In many parts of the country the number of cattle is so small, in proportion to the quantity of herbage, that much of the grass remains neither depastured nor cut; and it is a common practice to set fire to the dry grass which is in this state in the spring, in order to prevent the rotting of the roots. The alluvial prairies are generally to be found on the margins of the rivers, and they are of a deep pliable soil of extraordinary fertility.

During the months of vegetation, no adequate idea can be formed of the number, form, varieties, and hues of the flowering plants and shrubs of the prairies. In spring, the prevalent colour of the prairie flowers is bluish-purple; in midsummer, red, with a considerable proportion of yellow; and in autumn, the flowers are very large, and so many of them of the helianthus form, that the prairie receives from them quite a splendid covering of yellow.

In many of the extensive prairies in Louisiana and elsewhere, there are what are called islands of wooded land. They generally have an appearance of such beauty, and are so well placed, that a stranger is with difficulty convinced that they are not clumps of trees planted out in circular, square, or triangular forms, for the beauty of their appearance. It is impossible to convey to one who has not seen it any idea of the effect produced by one of these circular clumps of trees, rising like a tower from the smooth surface of a verdant plain. Wherever a streamlet crosses the prairie, it is marked with a fringe of trees, which very much increases the variety of the scenery.

There are few roads yet made in the prairie land, but, as the prairies are only to be found in the warm climates of the south and the west, where the soil is seldom wet for any long period, the tracts of road are almost at all times good, except in the low lands, or swamps by the river sides. Indeed, in many parts of the dry prairies where I travelled, the roads were as smooth as those which are generally to be found formed covered with small broken stones and gravel in an English park, and had very much the same appearance.

After a charming drive we arrived, with a keen appetite for breakfast, at a small cabin kept by a person of the name of Bonum.

6

Anne Royall

Spring 1830

Anne Newport Royall (1769–1854), after a secure and privileged married life of twenty-six years, found herself widowed and financially ruined at fifty-four. She decided to support herself by writing about her travels and the people she met. Eventually, she wrote about, or at least mentioned, almost two thousand Americans, and in doing so became a national figure. The public either adored or despised her for her blatant prejudices and approval of her "friends" or vindictive denunciations of those who were not so graced. Her accounts are generally accurate.

She was against Evangelical Christians, attempts to prohibit Sabbath transportation and mail service, the United States Bank, and nullification; she was for tolerance of Roman Catholics, separation of church and state, Masons, sound money, states' rights regarding slavery, internal improvements, and government support for scientific research. Mrs. Royall judged others based on her prejudices, but primarily on how they received or avoided her; she was easily offended and not at all reticent about excoriating individuals by name and in print. She was also obsessed with individuals' personal appearances. She carried her self-published books with her. Perhaps fear of being published in one of Mrs. Royall's subsequent books also intimidated those who crossed her path. Today, this self-important and self-absorbed woman would be a television celebrity. Nevertheless, reading through her prejudices and her self-absorption, and savoring her idiosyncratic spellings and punctuation, Mrs. Royall's books are informative of a young United States. The woman herself is a character worthy of Dickens.

Anne Royall, ***Mrs. Royall's Southern Tour, or Second Series of the Black Book,***

3 vols. (Washington: self-published, 1831), II:180–189.

Having received a polite invitation from Major Johnston of Montgomery, to make his house my home, I did not stop at the tavern, but drove directly to Major Johnston's. Mrs. Johnston, (who is a sister of my friend Mrs. Greer of Washington City,) happened to be out—but the door was no sooner opened by a servant, than the driver spoke and said, "there is Mrs. J. now." She had been on a visit, and hearing I had proceeded to her house hastened home and gave me a cordial welcome.

She led me through an elegant parlor, dining room, and thence into a neat chamber which contained one of those snowy beds, "this is your parlor Mrs. R., here you eat, and here you sleep; make yourself at home." Major Johnston I had seen at Washington City, but Mrs. Johnston never before.

At Montgomery I took leave of Capt. Walker's line, intending to go to Mobile by water, which lay on my way to New Orleans. In justice to Capt. Walker, his drivers, horses, and coaches, are exceeded by none on the line. The Capt. was at Mobile attending the trial of Tuskeena, the chief who stopped the mail. I therefore missed the pleasure of seeing him altogether, as he had left Mobile before I reached there.

I took Mrs. Johnston's advise and was perfectly at home, though I only intended to spend the night there, as I never stop at private houses, on many accounts, no matter how kind my entertainers may be. Mrs. Johnston is one of your stout, jolly, liberal, sensible women, untainted with tracts or missionaries. She is older than Mrs. Greer, though still young and lively. She was pleased to see any one from Washington, who could converse with her about her sister, to whom she is much attached. She has a handsome fair face, and gay, open benevolent countenance, and resembles her sister in her unbounded charity to the poor.

We walked in the garden, and to the Alabama river, upon the bank of which her house stood, and the evening being cool, roved about every where, looking at the town, the river and the country.

I was much gratified to reach this wealthy State once more, though I had never been so far south. Not only wealthy, but the handsomest in the Union.

After awhile the Major came, and also desired me to consider myself at home. They have no children, the house therefore was exactly to my taste.

One or two gentlemen called that evening, one an inmate of the family, Mr. Whetman, was all joy at my arrival, and I was quite at home, with his polite, frank, and friendly manners, and took up a favorable opinion of the town. Retiring to my chamber, Mrs. Johnstone, who owns a handsome property in Washington City, came in, and we had a long chat about that and other things. I also received several ladies, late as the hour was.

Next morning, I made myself easy as to other quarters, until I saw some friend. Hearing a steam-boat was going to Mobile, the next day, I determined to proceed in it. I was rather hurt however, to see Major Johnston making preparations for a large company, wines, liquors, &c. I was determined it should not be on my account; though probably it might have been the same every day. Meantime, several gentlemen came in, whom the Major introduced as his friends. My friend Whitman, who called over night, scarcely left the room at all.

It was not long however, before one of the Majors' friends indulged in liberties which I do not allow, and reproved him very promptly, which the Major seemed to resent. I had a great deal to do, and but a short time to accomplish it in; the Majors house too, being far from the business part of the town, I soon came to a point. I did not know a single soul in the place, but calling a very decent gentleman into another room, I desired him to do me the favor to go and bring one or two of the Masons to me, as I knew they were every where. The gentleman, (whose name I do not know) deserves eternal honor for his kindness. I then returned to the company, and no one suspected me. In a few minutes a man of incomparable sweetness of aspect, came in with one or two others. The gentleman drew up towards me, with his hat in his hand, his face covered with blushes, partly hid by his black clustering locks. I saw at once he was the friend I stood in need of. He was by my side on the sofa in an instant, and said "I am one of the gentlemen you sent for, how can I serve you?" I am mostly attended by three or four, and asked "if there were any more of my friends present"—"Yes" he said "there is one looking at you." I looked up and saw a fine gentleman, eyeing me with deep attention. I was not astonished at this, as it is common, but thought it odd he should not approach and speak to me—"Oh he will presently," said Dr. Hoxey, the gentleman sitting by me. I then gave Dr. H. a summary of my wishes, alternately replying to the addresses of the company, which by this time grew numerous. The tall gentleman mentioned, remained standing, supporting himself carelessly upon the bureau, resting his head upon his hand, with his eye steadily bent on me. He also had addressed me respecting my tour, and seemed rather pointed; I replied to him as I did to the rest, very promptly, and the moment Dr. Hoxey, got up, he came and seated himself in the Dr's. place and taking hold of my hand, pressed it with great ardour. "I never was more prejudiced against a person in my life, Mrs. Royall, than I was against you, until I saw you, said the gentleman," I find you quite a different woman from what you were represented—I have been grossly imposed upon, you are not the same woman at all I expected: I soon discovered that, and now esteem you as much as I detested you before." "Why sir, who has slandered me to you, who could know me here, I never was in this part of the State." "Oh every body, travellers from months past, supposing you would come this way, represented you in such terms, that I actually said if you were to come into my house, I would kick you out." "These must have been the missionaries," said I. "Yes, they were, and other ruffians whom you would not admit to see you. The ruffian as you justly called him, who came on in the stage with you, said every thing infamous of you, and when I heard you wished to see some of the towns people, and Hoxey called for me, I came with him to be sure, but not with any friendly intention at all—they charged you with every thing.— In the whole creation does there exist such monsters or wickedness! worse than pirates—worse than midnight assassins, for they only take your life—but these missionary monsters take your character, dearer than all. "But why, dear sir do you credit report, you know it is for the most part false:" "it is wrong I know, and am more convinced of it now than ever."—His name is Freeman, a man of wealth, and the co.owner of an extensive tavern, though he lived private himself. After requesting to know how he could serve me, he and Dr. H. retired into another room, and after consulting together, one of them came to the door and called me in: we have attended to your wishes madam, you go to my house, I am part owner of the tavern you saw, there are several empty room, take your choice and look upon me as your friend. The Dr. here and myself will attend you any moment—"are you ready" "I am" leaving my baggage, which Mr. Freeman promised to send for. I merely told Mrs. J. I was going to take a walk, which was no story. I took the arm of the adored Freeman, and walked to the tavern; all this was the business of a very few minutes, and so secretly done (as we spoke low) that not one of a large party knew any thing of it; and least of all the Major and his lady, until they saw me take the arm of the gentleman. The whole party followed, forming a pretty respectable escort.

Most of these were aware of Mr. Freeman's prejudice—even that morning, they heard him utter many, and very unfriendly expressions toward me; imagine their surprise, to see him paying the most decided and affectionate attention. "You are doubtless astonished, gentlemen, but I must yield to truth—I can never do enough to repair the injury I have done this lady." The dear Hoxey, too, walked on the other side, and thus shielded by merit and friendship, I asked no boot of the world. In a few minutes, I was seated in a large, cool parlor on the lower floor, with a comfortable chamber adjoining; and my friends were brought in, sometimes by Mr. F., the bar-keeper, the Dr., and Mr. Whitman.

I shall nevertheless cherish a high sense of gratitude toward Major Johnston and his lady, and from the first resolved not to impose upon their generosity; and the probability is, I might have had some difficulty had it not been for them. For though my letters were a sufficient safeguard, one might suffer a great deal before reference could be had to them. His house was quite too far from the town.

Montgomery, like the towns on the frontier of Georgia, has great advantages. It is at the head of steamboat navigation, though steamboats go up to the Falls of the Coosy, several miles above the town. It is surrounded on all sides with fertile land, all in cultivation. It stands on the great mail route from Washington City to New Orleans, via Mobile, and in the vicinity of a number of flourishing towns on the Alabama. It occupies a high bluff which commands an extensive view of the rich lands, watered by the river. The finest body of land in the State, viz. the *Great Bend*, is adjoining the town. This bend nearly circles an extensive plain of amazing fertility. The boats are seen making their circle round it from the bluff. It is most beautiful, smooth, deep stream, navigable from the falls to Mobile, 512 miles, without the least obstruction. The prospect from the bluff, is one of vast extent and incomparable beauty.

The town lies partly on even ground, while some of the houses spread out upon an eminence, on the opposite side to the river. The streets are wide and regular, and the principal are beautifully shaded, with the pride of China. It contains a Court-house, prison, one old Church, and a very handsome *Theatre*, well done.—The people have some sense here. It contains between 8 and 900 inhabitants,—I saw the old church, and the hypocrites can't raise money enough to repair it. But they are gaining ground fast; they have just established a Sunday-school, and a newspaper.* They are violently opposed, however, by the citizens, who are well-informed, and enlightened people

One Beecher, a stout black-smith, a nephew of Dr. Beecher's of Boston, and a very fine fellow, too, amused me no little with anecdotes of his uncle, sending bundles and boxes of tracts to him. There are a great many goats in Montgomery, and Mr. Beacher would catch the goats, and stick a tract on each horn, and send them forth to spread the gospel—much honester Missionaries, I must confess, and much more respectable, that the two-legged Missionaries—these told no lies. The mischievous wag, he must have a fertile imagination, to think of such a thing. The whole town was in a roar of laughter: thus those swindlers bring their trade into contempt. To return, Montgomery has a Library; 7 Lawyers; 5 Doctors; and exported 1200 bales of cotton, the previous year. Two newspapers are published here.

Many of the houses are large, and well-built, of brick. The town does much retail business, and is inhabited by intelligent, and high-minded men. The wealthiest people in the State, however, are the planters, who reside on their plantations. These, however, are often in the towns, and with a regular Thespian society, and now and then a company, balls and parties, the citizens contrive to amuse themselves with all deference to the tracts.

* Royall's note: The latter has since walked off, for want of patronage.

It is a perfect thorough-fare of travellers.

Dr. Noodle, lives not far from this place—I mean in the county of Pike: he was one that brought on a shocking account of me. But I have fixed his Noodleship as long as he lives—nothing like truth to indure.

Nearly every one in the town came to see me, and a number of those (for the time) from the country, my friends, Dr. H. and Mr. F. I have mentioned: nor could any description, I have given depict their character, in more glowing colors, than the generous act already related. Mr. Freeman, as I said, is a tall, elegant figure, with a good, fair face, mild, steady countenance, and soft blue eye. His manners are what his actions, bespeak prompt and friendly: he watched over me like another guardian angel, often coming in to know, if I lacked any thing. Obliged to leave the place before I did, he came into the room and said, "I am obliged to leave you, but here is my partner, Mr. Stevens, he will attend to you in my place, and you may rely upon him." Mr. S. bowed an assent: nor did I ever press a hand more fervently, nor have I ever seen a man more worthy the character of a gentleman—I hope my friends, which are numerous, may reward him. Mr. F. was married to the cousin, or perhaps the sister of Governor Bibb: she was indisposed, but I got a glimpse of her after Mr. F departed; she was a modest, sweet, pretty woman, and as much to be envied as Dr. Bird, though she is doubtless as amiable as her husband.

Dr. Asa Hoxey, is rather of a low stature, but keenly made: his face is round, full and handsome, with one of the most expressive black eyes in human head. His fine, deep forehead is adorned with a profusion of black, glossy hair; but to describe his countenance, would be to paint the sun—the portrait of charity. Nor did ever the appearance and actions of a man, so perfectly correspond. He is quite a young man, stands high as a physician. It would be criminal to say more of mortal, though I could fill a volume, and the half would be untold.

George Whitman, Esq. is a very young man, and not at all behind the others in generosity; but he was not a *mason*—he laughed, however, and said, "I was born a mason, Mrs. Royall, I love them as well as you do." He certainly is immeasurably kind, and one of the whole soul sort. He is a Yankee, has been sometime in the south, and universally esteemed.

Mr. W. is at the head of the thespian society, and said, "the godly ones wanted to buy the theatre for a church, but if they do, they shall pay for it, Mrs. Royall"—he would never give up the theatre. He is a light, genteel figure, with handsome, oval features, and sparkling eye—his countenance is open and gay, and his manners polished and familiar. He may be called the Chesterfield of Montgomery, and the ladies are all fond of him. My visit happened at an unlucky time—the principal part of the gentlemen were at Washington Court, to hear an interesting trial, and I *never* wait.

I had seen a Mr. Lynch, from Washington, at Washington city—he was very friendly there, and invited me to call at Washington, Alabama, by all means. I had sent word to him by Mr. Matthews, I would be glad to see him, and that, as there was no alternative, if he would make some arrangement, I would visit Washington and wait there for the steamboat. He never came, nor did he write; but he had married a wife since I saw him, and is, no doubt, another addition to the henpecked corps, or something worse.

I have often seen southern ladies, married to Yankee gentlemen, but here I found a southern gentleman married to a Yankee lady. This was Wm. D. Pickett, Esq., an Attorney, a tall, genteel, young, friendly man, married to a young lady of Rhode Island. I admired his taste, a Yankee girl is a fortune herself. She was very handsome, sprightly and accomplished—they were very equally matched.

I likewise found other Yankee ladies there, one in particular, whom I had seen in Haverhill, N.H.

A Mr. Herbert, an Editor, was pretty clever, and who should call amongst the rest, but Mr. *Sayer*, my old fellow-traveller, and likewise his sister, who left me at Macon. She had a dreadful time of it the next night—it was quite an adventure, they were overtaken by a thunder-storm, and being dark, the driver lost the road, and the stage became so much entangled in the brush, he had to take a horse and ride 6 miles for a light—and the Scotchman, instead of remaining with her in the stage, to protect her from the Missionaries, and other wild beasts, went with the driver! Was there ever such a fool! While he was gone, the Missionary in the stage converted the young lady! This is the way they take the advantage of our women!—she was a very handsome, and a very intelligent lady, but she will soon join the church now. There was a third, P. D. Sayre, Esq., the best looking of the whole, and a very fine man.

One Mr. Walton, who boarded at the tavern, said, "he was the grandson of one of the signers of the Declaration of Independence." He was a tall, rather handsome man, and an old bachelor, though he could not be said to be old: what his christian name was, heaven knows, the initials are J. K. T. D. W.—he was rather a quiz, and not very pleasant.

Mr. *Thompson*, the tract Editor, said he thought "the tracts saved souls,"—then money can save souls, as the tracts arise from money. I asked him what became of the souls of those who died before tracts were made?—He was silent. Some of these ruffians sent a negro in to me with a tract—I told the negro to be gone, or I would have him whipped—"be gone, and give it to those who sent you." The fellow scared out of his wits, ran for his life—he was told, I would give him 25cts.

Mr. Bell, the Sheriff, is a stout, fine-looking man, and hates tracts. Mr. M'Bride mentioned, was his deputy.

Mr. *Prichard* is a great wag, and amused me with a description of the sharpers who fled to this wealthy State on its first settlement. He said, "there was the plain Yankee; he was a gentleman: then there was the Yankee *Doodle*; he took the filling out of the shirt: then the Yankee Doodle Dandy; he took the whole—and the Irish Jew took the skin with it. They call him the Preacher. He said, "I ring the Church bell, but never go into the Church. Whenever these fellows come round me, Mrs. R., I always jump right upon them rough-shod. Colonel Charles Hooks is amongst the first gentlemen in the town. He is a tall slender man of elegant manners; he was formerly of Wilmington, and is a very pleasant man. Mr. Stevens, the partner of my friend, is a small young man of very amiable manners, no way behind his partner in merit or modesty.

I had several calls from gentlemen from the country—both gentlemen and ladies; all curious to see the woman who wrote the Black Book. Of these, Judge King, Col. Cook, and family, were distinguished. Judge *King* is quite a splendid man. He is a stout middle-aged man, erect and tall, with a large full face, ruddy complexion, and fine full grey eyes; his manners are of the first order—refined and dignified. Col. *Cook* is also one of the great men of the State. Mrs. *Cook*: it had been some time since I saw Alabama ladies, and was no less gratified with her than those in North Alabama. She was a young handsome woman, of highly polished manners, with that charm and easy grace which distinguish the ladies of the South; she was attended by her son and daughter, both modest and deeply interesting. Dr. *Holt* and a Mr. *Pond* called, whether of the town or country I do not know. Dr. Holt is a young man, with a good figure and fair oval face, and a genteel man. Mr. P. looked rather solemn; he must be of the pious party.

I find Mr. Clay has several friends here; most of them *simpletons, broken down* politicians, *broken* merchants, tract and bible, and rope people. Some of my greatest friends are Clay men; but I happened to have none amongst these but the Sayers. I shall let the Postmaster, Black and Blue, stand till I find the $40 stolen from the mail somewhere there or here abouts.

Meantime my friend, Mrs. Johnston, paid me the most assiduous attention; she came often to see me, and overhauled my wardrobe, and had me neatly rigged up for my voyage down the river; she was kind to the last.

On the 3d day of my arrival, (having spend one day and a half at Montgomery,) my friends having engaged a passage to Mobile in the Steamboat *Herald*, Capt. *Young*—attended by a friend, I went on board. The boat was soon visited by my friends, and many of the citizens, whom I had not seen. I was introduced to the Captain, a noble fine fellow, and a *Mason*. Heaven always puts me in their care; also one of the owners of the boat, John P. Degarnett, Esq. a most worthy man. Mr. D. is of Swiss descent, and a gentleman of considerable wealth, pleasing and affable in his deportment. He is of middle age, with a round full face, soft grey eye, and very expressive countenance. I should say he was another Wm. Gaston, from what I saw. He is much beloved in Montgomery. Also James T. Degarnett, Esq., no less amiable.

With these came my friend Dr. Hoxey, Messrs. J. T. Camp, (of Columbus, Geo.,) Cornelius Robinson, Wm. Peacock, and S. Pollard, and a Mr. Powell, whom, it appears, I saw at Richmond, Va. Mr. P. is a warm hearted amiable man.

I was pleased to meet with Mr. Camp for the sake of Columbus, and pleased with the others for their own sakes. Nor did they forget I had a long tour before me. May heaven reward them! For nothing short of heaven can! My favorite Whitman too. This was the best collection I had seen; all choice spirits. Besides these I had a levee of ladies on board—I was proud of Alabama, my favorite State—these were Mrs. Johnston and Cook, and Miss Cook; the dear Mrs. J. hung to me to the last.

The boat having still some of her lading to take in, we enjoyed ourselves till she had finished. At length the fire was put to the engine, the steam began to hiss, and the bell to ring; my friends having done all they could do, came forward, and the parting pangs succeeded, and in a few minutes we were under way.

DOWN ALABAMA RIVER.

From the day I left Alabama till I returned to it, I have seen no state or country equal to it. The people wealthy and generous, the land rich, the fields large, its rivers deep and smooth, its lofty bluffs, its majestic trees, its dark green forests, is altogether grand.

Alabama river is 200 yards wide at Montgomery, and was quite low. It was about sun down when we left Montgomery; this grieved me, as the boat went all night, and I should lose much of the beauty of the scenery, which is very different from that more South. The foliage here is black green, and consists of tree and vine. Every tree is clothed in vines, which run up to the top, and hangs from thence to the water in dense clusters. This vine has a large blue flower; other trees again have their trunks only wrapped in green by a slender vine of most prolific foliage. Its leaves consist of layers so deep, that the body of the trees which it delights in most, is completely swathed in green. In many places those vines are of such exuberance and weight, they bend the top of the tree; again the vine ascends to the top, and seizing upon every limb and twig, wraps the whole of it in the richest dress. This has no comparison in beauty. These and the bluffs amused me till it grew very dark, being cloudy.

We stopped at Washington to take in freight. It is only eleven miles below Montgomery.

7

Thomas Hamilton

April 1831

THOMAS HAMILTON (1789–1842), although the son of a Scottish professor of anatomy and botany, was not himself destined for the academic life. After studying for three years at Glasgow University, he secured an army commission in 1810. He served in the Peninsula Campaign against Napoleon's armies, was seriously wounded, and after subsequent service in Canada and the occupation of France, retired as a captain in 1818. Hamilton, who worked on the periphery of the literary world, knew Wordsworth, Scott, and Carlyle and published minor works, including a novel: *Men and Manners in America* was so popular that it was translated into French and German within ten years of its publication. He is humorous in his criticism of the United States and the South, as is evident in the following passage, but his criticism is fair, if superficial. He was strongly opposed to slavery.

Thomas Hamilton, *Men and Manners in America* (Philadelphia: Cary, Lea and Blanchard, 1833), 332–335.

On the 15th of April I embarked on board of the steam-boat Isabella, bound up the Alabama river for Montgomery. As there were no ladies on board, my English friend and myself succeeded in getting possession of the cabin usually appropriated for their accommodation. Our apartment was immediately above that occupied by the gentlemen, and being surrounded by a balcony, it was impossible to desire any thing more agreeable. The party below seemed to consist almost exclusively of farmers, who, though exceedingly offensive both in habits and deportment, are yet a shade better that the inhabitants of towns. There is nothing *rustic*, however, about any

American; nothing of that simplicity which distinguishes the peasantry of other countries. The eye is almost uniformly expressive of care and cunning; and often, as I looked on the furrowed and haggard countenances which surrounded the dinner table, have I asked myself, "Is it possible that these men make pretension to happiness?"

In my progress down the western waters, I had become accustomed to a table, loaded even to excess with provisions of all sorts. In the Southern States there is no such profusion. Our dinners on board the Isabella were scanty in quantity, and far from laudable of the score of quality. Plates, dishes, knives and forks, tablecloths, all were dirty and disgusting. But bating these disagreeables, our voyage was pleasant and prosperous. The Alabama is a river apparently about the size of the Hudson; and the scenery through which it led us, was very pleasing, though deficient in variety. Either bank presented a splendid mass of luxuriant foliage, and some of the noblest timber I had ever seen. Among the forest trees I remarked the plane, the cotton-tree, dogwood, oak of several varieties, magnolia grandiflora, maple, gum-tree, hackberry, &c. At night I was peculiarly struck with the beauty of the stars reflected in the pure waters of the river. The whole sky was mirrored with a vividness which exceeded every thing of the kind I have ever witnessed before or since.

In the evening we passed Claiborne, a pretty village on a height, a short distance from the river. In a State so thinly peopled as Alabama, however, it is talked of as a considerable place; but from all I saw or heard of it, Claiborne is not increasing, nor is it likely to increase. On the morning following, we came to Portland, a miserable place, consisting of a store and a few wretched houses. This is what is called in American phrase, "a great improvement." We called at every house in the place in search of milk, but could get none.

Our next stoppage was at Cahawba, which, a year or two back, was the seat of government of the State. It is a very poor collection of very poor houses, not, I should imagine, above twenty in number. The Court-house happening to be open, I entered, and found the Court engaged in the discharge of business. On the elevated platform, composed of rough unpainted boards, sat his honour, the judge, not better dressed, and apparently somewhat filthier in habits, than an English ploughman. The case concerned the payment of a doctor's bill: the counsel for defendant, a gentleman in a fustian jacket, was in the act of addressing the Court. He read an act of the legislature, enacting that no practitioner of the healing art should recover for medical attendance, without having been previously licensed by a Board of Doctors, and called on the plaintiff, as a necessary preliminary, to produce his certificate.

This was evidently inconvenient, and the plaintiff's counsel, whose appearance seemed to indicate a combination of the trade of blacksmith with that of barrister, was somewhat taken aback by the demand. The learned gentleman, however, attempted with all his ingenuity, to get out of the scrape, and at the conclusion of every sentence, hitched up his corduroy breeches, which seemed in danger of dropping about his heels, with a grace peculiarly his own. Unfortunately I had not time to wait for the peroration of the speech. The steam-boat bell sounded, and no time was to be lost in getting on board.

Shortly after dark we reached Selma, the most considerable settlement on the Alabama, between Mobile and Montgomery. There was no quay, and a good deal of the cargo was rolled out upon the bank without any one to receive it. I did not see Selma, for the night was cloudy and moonless, and the village stands a short distance from the river.

On the fourth day, our voyage terminated. Montgomery is what is called "a considerable place," though its population does not exceed a few hundreds, and these exclusively of the poorer order. There is not one tolerable house, and nothing could be worse than the inn. In the way of dormitory, nothing was to be had but a room with three beds in it, all of which were destined to be occupied. What was still worse, the beds were full of vermin, and the moschetoes more annoying than I had yet found them.

In such circumstances I was up with the lark, and set out on a long ramble through the neighbouring country. The soil is poor and light, but presents a prettily undulating surface. From one height I enjoyed a fine view of the river, which is truly, even at this distance from the sea, a noble object. After a walk of three hours I returned to the inn, having fortunately succeeded in throwing off by exercise, the fever and fatigue of the restless night.

In the Southern States, there is little of that stirring spirit of improvement so apparent in the regions of the West. The towns and villages are without appearance of business, and the number of dilapidated—if the word may be applied to structures of wood—houses, indicates a decreasing, rather than an augmenting population. In Montgomery, many houses had been deserted, and the Court-house seemed fast falling into decay.

At four o'clock P. M., we started in the mail stage for Fort Mitchell.

8

Sol Smith

January 1830, January–June 1835

Solomon Franklin Smith (1801–1869), a native of New York State who had only a rudimentary education, was attracted to the theater in his mid-teens and read Shakespeare on his own. In his mid-twenties he became a professional actor and theatrical manager. By his mid-thirties he was a comedic star, playing in New York, Philadelphia, St. Louis, Mobile, and Montgomery. From 1835 until 1853, theatrical managers Noah Ludlow and Sol Smith dominated the theaters of St. Louis, Mobile, and New Orleans—and the entire Western region. In 1853, Smith left the stage and became a St. Louis lawyer. Serving in the Missouri State Convention in 1861, he helped keep Missouri from seceding from the Union.

The Theatrical Journey is one of Smith's three autobiographical works. The following passage illustrates the values of the antebellum actor-manager: fun-loving and amused by the absurdities of life, as well as attached to those he played with and who befriended him as he traveled from stage to stage.

Sol Smith, *The Theatrical Journey—Work and Anecdotical Recollections of Sol Smith* (Philadelphia: T. B. Peterson and Brothers, 1854), 44–47 and 174–178.

. . . receiving from MONTGOMERY a warm invitation to visit that town, and occupy for a limited period a beautiful new theatre, just erected by a Thespian Society, instead of taking a boat for Mobile, on our way to Natchez, (through New Orleans,) we once more betook ourselves to the large road wagons, and in five days found ourselves, "bag and baggage," at the place which is now the seat of government of Alabama.

Here I became acquainted with John H. Thorington, a lawyer of great practice, who possessed all the qualities requisite to constitute a good man. He is no longer living to read my praises; but it affords me a melancholy pleasure to record his unvarying kindness to me and mine. As mayor or intendant of the town, some years afterwards, he took a decided stand against the *gamblers* who congregated in Montgomery, in great force, and he was persecuted by them in various ways, until he concluded to leave the place, and remove to the western country. In Iowa he was afflicted with a disease consequent upon the severe climate, which settled into his limbs, causing paralysis, and threatening his life. In hopes of relief, he was taken to New Orleans, and placed as a boarder in the Charity Hospital, where he ended his days. I was with him while he was lying on his death-bed, and afforded him at least the satisfaction of knowing he had a friend near him. Poor Thoringon! He could not *speak* his thanks; but the pressure of his hand, even after he had lost the ability to raise his arm, told me that his stout Irish heart retained its warmth to the last pulsation.

There were other warm and true friends that I made in Montgomery—George Whitman, for one. At the time I write this, Mr. Whitman was one of the first merchants of the place, and owned real estate sufficient to make him a millionaire, which he would undoubtedly be at this moment—*if he had held on to it.*

The MONTGOMERY THEATRE opened, in an unfinished state, the latter part of January, 1830. The attendance was good for two weeks, which was the limit of our stay, in consequence of my engagement at Natchez. Madame Feron, the great singer, performed with us two nights, and as we were without a regular orchestra, various means were resorted to for an accompaniment to her songs. A piano-forte was introduced upon the stage, and she accompanied herself in some pieces—in others, she pressed me into the service. Thus in the farce entitled, "Of Age to-morrow," the dialogue was necessarily changed a little from the original text:

Maria—I had a lover once.

Baron—A lover? Twenty, I dare say.

Maria—But he deserted me.

Baron—Deserted you? Impossible? What had he to say for himself?

Maria—He said nothing; but [if you'll have the kindness to seat yourself at that piano, and give me an accompaniment] I'll tell you what I said to him."

Suiting the action to the word, the accomodating Baron Willinghurst (personated by the writer hereof,) seated himself at the piano, and the beautiful song, "As I hang on your bosom," was gloriously breathed forth by the great prima donna of European Opera, in a theatre surrounded by uncut trees, and occupied by an audience whose appreciation was as warm as that of the dilettanti of Italy. In the farce of "No Song no Supper," to account for the presence, in *Farmer Crop's* house, of so rich an article of furniture as a piano-forte, *Crop* was constrained to say that a rich neighbour has *stored* it *there* until he could get his new house ready for its reception. Thus accounting for the instrument being there, it was an easy matter to ask *Margaretta* to *play upon it*—then a *song* was asked for; and after that another, and so on. Madame Feron entered into the spirit of the scene, and seemed to enjoy herself very much, imparting her good humour to all around, both before and behind the curtain. Mr. Maddox, since manager of the Princess Theatre, London, accompanied Madame Feron, as her man of business. From Montgomery she proceeded to New Orleans, where she had an engagement.

In the two weeks we received in Montgomery the sum of $883, out of which I paid Madame Feron $101 for her two nights acting and singing.

At the moment of departure from this village, I had a pleasant interview with Mr. Thomas S. Hamblin, who was returning from a southern engagement. While revising these pages, I hear of his decease!

We proceeded next to SELMA, a very small village on the Alabama river, where we performed nine nights in a ball room, fitted up for the purpose, to receipts of exactly $70 per night. The number of inhabitants did not exceed 400, white, black, and children. Those who visited the theatre, visited it *every* night. The sheriff, being one day compelled to leave town on business, came and *left his dollar* at the bar of the hotel where we performed!

Arrived at Mobile . . .

. . . Deciding to make directly for Montgomery, without stopping at Macon and Columbus, we made arrangements for our journey of three hundred miles, which we accomplished, after undergoing unheard-of hardships, in ten days, at an expense not much short of $1000, without reckoning the salaries of the company. At Caleba Swamp, we found about three thousand persons waiting for the mending of a bridge. If any one is curious to know some of the incidents at this "watering place," let him purchase J. M. Field's "Drama at Pokerville," and turn to the sketch entitled, "A Night in a Swamp."

Opened at MONTGOMERY on the 3d of January, 1835, with the "Heir at Law" and "'Tis All a Farce." Next night we played "Hamlet" and "My Aunt"—*Hamlet*, Mr. J. M. Field, who, the reader must know, had been during the preceding year "doing up" the leading business of tragedy very acceptably to the Georgians. I can never consider Mr. Field a great *tragedian;* but I do say that I have seen many much worse representatives of *King Lear, Richard, Othello, Sir Giles Overreach, Shylock,* and *Hamlet,* than he was at the time I am writing of. At *this* time he occasionally "goes on" for *Claude Melnotte* and *Sir Thomas Clifford*; but the opinion seems to be quite prevalent among the "b-hoys" that "Jo has better stick to comedy."

During this season, Mrs. Drake acted with us a starring engagement—so did Yankee Hill, and—last, not least—HENRY J. FINN. I remember seeing him play *Iago* at the old Chatham Theatre in 1824. He was now a comedian—and *such* a comedian!

Urged by the citizens of WETUMPKA, I sent my dramatic forces, under the temporary command of Brev. Gen. J. M. Field, so that remarkably primitive city, where a considerable business was done in a billiard room, hastily transformed into a theatre, during a season of two weeks. MR. CHARLES MASON, a nephew of John Kemble, played here three or four nights, to good houses.

HAYNEVILLE, in the opposite direction, now claimed a visit; and in a large room in the academy, a little out of town, the drama shed forth its influences on audiences who gave no token whatever of their appreciation of our efforts. For twelve successive nights we exerted ourselves for their edification; and to this day I am in utter ignorance whether our efforts were satisfactory or not—for not a hand of applause greeted us during the whole time; neither did a smile—a laugh was out of the question—shed its ray, to cheer us on in our task. Yes—there *was* one attempt at a slight smile—indeed, I might say that a real jolly laugh was on the point of breaking out on one occasion; but it was checked in its incipiency. It was during the performance of the "Hypocrite," Act V., where *Macworm* mounts on a table behind a screen and gives an extemporaneous discourse, which on this particular occasion was interlarded with some local hits, which actually took effect upon one tall fellow sanding in a corner near the stage. A premature "Ha! ha! h"—was just bursting out, when one of the deacons of the Presbyterian Church arose from a chair with great solemnity, and addressed the *quasi* disturber of the assembly thus: Mr. Thompson, you must quit that or leave the meeting." Mr. Thompson "shut up."

"Old Jack Barnes," with his wife, and daughter Charlotte, came to play an engagement towards the end of the season, in Montgomery, opening in the "School for Scandal," in the first scene of the second act of which, a fat negro wench, being told to hold up Miss Barnes' train until she got to the wing, *followed that lady on the stage*, and remained there, holding up the train, during the ceremony of reception, which, under the circumstances, was an uproarious one—and reluctantly leaving, with a low curtsy, only when Sir Peter (Mr. Barnes) told her that her services were no longer required.

On one of "Yankee Hill's" nights, (with shame I confess it,) my name was associated with his in the committal of a horrid murder!—*Richard* and *Richmond* being the characters in which we perpetrated the dreadful deed.

Our prompter's name was Gay. He performed old men, personated marble statues, and danced comic hornpipes. On one occasion, the performances ending with "Don Juan," in which Gay enacted the part of the murdered governor on horseback, (a statue,) the audience demanded a *comic dance* before they would leave the house.

"What is to be done?" asked Gay, in a piteous tone, the perspiration bursting out through the Spanish whiting on his face. "It will take at least a quarter of an hour to prepare for a dance!"

"Not at all," replied I, promptly; "go on as you are."

"What!" said Gay, "go on for a comic dance dressed as a marble statue?"

"Yes—as the marble statue; it will be all the more comic,"—and up went the curtain.

The audience relished the dance hugely; and I must say that the marble statue, dancing to the tune of "a frog he would a-wooing go," *was* a most original and mirth-provoking affair.

During the engagement of the Barnes', we performed the farce of "Three Weeks after Marriage." It will be remembered that there is in this piece a matrimonial quarrel about a game of cards. A fellow in the pit had listened to the dispute with much interest until the end of the first act, when, just before the fall of the drop, *Sir Charles*, in reply to his lady's invitation to go to bed, exclaims—"I'll not go to bed with any woman who don't know what's trumps." The man in the pit got up in utter surprise, and said, in a tone loud enough to be heard by the whole house—"Well, you're a cursed fool to quarrel about such a trifle! Blast me if *I* wouldn't confess to the diamond, and go to bed!" The drop scene again rose, and soon the newly married couple were engaged in their dispute about the game of whist, and to convince his wife of her error, *Sir Charles* went up to the table and dealt out the cards. The man in the pit called out and asked "what's trumps?" Sir Charles just at that moment said "clubs!" and his lady "diamonds!" which appeared to be answers to his question; whereupon the auditor took up his hat and made for the door, exclaiming—"*I* shan't wait any longer; they've been quarrelling here for half an hour about clubs and diamonds—I don't see as there's any likelihood of their coming to an understanding, so I'll go; it's getting late." This speech elicited a round of applause from the pit. Turning as he was about passing through the opening into the passage, he addressed *Sir Charles* and *Lady Rackett*—"young people, you'd better make up that little difficulty and let the play go on—it's of mighty little consequence *what* was trumps; make it up and go to bed!" Then looking up at the audience, who were roaring with laughter, he made a low bow, and retired from sight, lit a cigar at a lamp in the passage, shook the door-keeper by the hand, and walked off.

Matthew Field, whom afterwards became a good actor, and somewhat celebrated as a writer, (under his own name and that of *Phazma*,) made his first appearance on any stage in Montgomery as *Hemeya*, in the tragedy of the "Apostate," Mrs. A. Drake performing *Florinda*. The debut was a successful one; but the "last scene of all in *that* eventful tragedy" was rendered somewhat ludicrously. If the reader is not aware of the fact, I must inform him that Mrs. Drake is what we term a *heavy* actress—(how well I remember her a slim young girl in Albany, thirty-eight years ago!)—and Florinda dies and *falls* beside Hemeya at the close of the piece. Mat. Field had got through *his* troubles, and lay dead and stiff, congratulating himself on the success he had met with on his first attempt at acting, when he suddenly perceived that Mrs. D. was preparing for "a fall" in the immediate vicinity of his own resting place. I was watching Mrs. D.'s splendid death, and it must be confessed that poor Mat. did appear in considerable danger of being *fallen upon* by the poisoned Florinda. At first there were sundry twitchings of the arms and legs of the dead Hemeya, then as the body of the devoted Florinda was seen actually descending, a sudden spring of her lover's corpse placed it out of danger, and there they both lay, "faithful to each other even in death." When Mat. found that he was not crushed, it seemed to occur to him that it was not altogether proper or picturesque to turn his back to the lady; so he very deliberately *turned over*, and stretching forth his dead arms, encircled her with them in a loving embrace, the curtain falling on the picture.

Mary Vos (afterwards Mrs. Stewart) performed a few nights, "previous to her departure for the eastern cities." This excellent actress and estimable woman is still a great favorite in Mobile, where she has reared and educated two lovely daughters, who, if they essay the stage, are destined to make a sensation in the theatrical world.

The season and my "country management," ended on the 10th of June, 1835, with my benefit, which was very largely attended, notwithstanding the extremely hot weather; my Montgomery friends, without resorting to the humbug of a "complimentary," filling the house to its utmost capacity, and cheering me with their shouts and kindly greetings to the last.

9

George Featherstonhaugh

January 1835

George William Featherstonhaugh (1780–1866), a British subject, served both the government of the United States and Great Britain. As United States geologist, he surveyed large portions of the West. His knowledge of the territory resulted in a British appointment to the commission to resolve the Anglo-American dispute about the Oregon Territory's northern border. Subsequently, he was appointed as a British consul in western France, where he died. His writings express the objectivity and interests of a scientific mind. Of course, it is not surprising that he disliked slavery and the slave trade or even that he was disgusted by American manners, but he also disapproved of democracy itself. He was positively impressed, however, by the South's physical resources.

Unlike most European travelers of the time, his travels were limited to the South. His son, who accompanied him, may have helped him recall his observations, but Featherstonhaugh himself keep daily notes, which he transcribed into his journal weekly.

G. W. Featherstonhaugh, *Excursion Through the Slave States,* (New York: Harper and Brothers, 1844), 144–145.

After a tolerably interesting and peaceful voyage [up the Alabama River from Mobile], we reached Montgomery in the afternoon of the 12th of January, and here the steamer was to stop some time. The Coosa was still navigable forty miles to Wetumpka, a place near the falls of the river, but the captain intending to remain some time here before he proceeded up, I determined to leave the boat. It would have been agreeable to me to have visited the falls, because, from the information I received, the rocks there were gneiss, and this was one of the points of limitation of the sedimentary beds, from which the ocean had last retired: besides, I heard that bituminous coal, which is also found on the Black Warrior and other parts of Alabama, existed on a partial line not far from the Wetumpka falls, which is exactly the manner in with the Chesterfield coal-field in Virginia is situated in relation to the falls on the James River at Richmond: and one of the interesting questions suggested by the geology of North America is as to whether there is a line of coal-fields in the United States east of the Alleghany mountains, running in detached basins from Virginia to Alabama. If the foliage had been out, the country would have been beautiful; but considering the softness of the climate here, and the great fertility of the soil in Alabama, it is not surprising that people should flock—as they do—to this favoured part of the United States. Still, with all its advantages, I must say that I would rather be a visiter than a sojourner in the land: the persecuting malaria, which never pardons the country a single season, is of itself a great objection, and the universal and extravagant use of tobacco by the people would be to me another of equal magnitude; so, what with the effluvia of nature and man combined, this fine country, with all its advantages, seems to fall very far short of a terrestrial Paradise.

I was glad to leave the boat, which was a very dirty concern, and nothing could be less tempting than our fare; some of the passengers were kind and communicative, but others were too fond of gambling, and spitting, and smoking to permit the enjoyment of much comfort. These were not Mobile people, but individuals going to different plantations, roads to which come out upon the river; and at most of these communications we either landed or took in persons on the way, but they were all coarse in their manners, and in many instances very disgusting. In an inordinate love of tobacco they all agreed, and it appeared to me that those whom the mania for this weed had seized in the strongest degree were always the most careless about their manners, as if it were out of character for a tobacco-eater to be decent. A few of the men employed on board the steamer were Muskogee, or Creek Indians; this was the first time I had seen aborigines employed as labourers, and from the activity they showed when we stopped to take in fuel, I could not but think that if a different policy had been observed towards this unfortunate race, good domestic servants and labourers might have been furnished from them in time, more intelligent than the negro, and fitted to the climate; but these considerations come too late—the fate of the Indians is sealed.

From the landing we had to walk a mile to Montgomery, a small straggling town with a population of from two to three thousand inhabitants, built upon a deposit of sand and red bluish clay, which, with occasional patches of rotten limestone in the local prairies of the neighbourhood, constitute the general soil of this part of the country.

The two principal streets are very broad, in the style common to all the southern towns, and from the great number of stores in them, amounting at least to one hundred, it would seem to be a place of extensive inland business; but of all the horrid filthy places into which I ever entered in any country, I think the *principal* hotel here, which was the one to which we were directed by common consent of all those we made inquiries of, bears the dirty palm. Everything about it seemed to breathe of whiskey and tobacco, and the walls of the bed-room to which I was shown were so incommunicably squirted over with a black-coloured tobacco-juice, and with more disgusting things, that it was evident the visitors to the place were, as to manners, but little raised above the inferior animals. There was an unfinished hotel then building opposite, but what the other hotels were which were not, "principal," I had not time to ascertain. I regretted much, however, that I had not gone to one of them, upon the very chance that they could not be worse, and might be better, following the principle that a gentleman of my acquaintance once pursued in writing from the country to his agent in New York: "The servants you have sent me with *good character* have all turned out so ill, that you will oblige me by sending those I am in want of at present with as little character as possible." And the plan succeeded for those with good characters thinking they could always get other places, did just as they pleased, whilst the others being anxious to keep their places, were more circumspect in their conduct.

There was little temptation to remain here, and I turned my attention to leaving the place as soon as I found out how uncomfortable it was likely to be. Upon inquiry I found that the roads through the Indian territory of the Creek nation, through which I had now to pass to get into the State of Georgia, were excessively broken up, especially the Indian bridges which cross the great swamps, and that in consequence thereof the letters were forwarded on horseback, the mail-coach being unable to run; so that I had got into a cleft stick, and must either remain here until the roads became passable for the mail—which was not expected until the spring—or must take a private conveyance and pay any price they might think proper to exact of me. The landlord was the person I had to deal with, and he ended a monstrous account of the difficulties with an equally monstrous price for conducting us in a miserable vehicle and a pair of wretched horses to Columbus, in Georgia, the distance being ninety miles. After a good deal of chaffering, I finally agreed to give him sixty-five dollars, which, with a gratuity to the driver, amounted to about four shillings a mile in English money.

10

Harriet Martineau

April 1835

HARRIET MARTINEAU (1802–1876) was not only a remarkable woman for her time, but a remarkable person for any time. Well-educated, she was freed to pursue her writing and intellectual interests when her family lost its fortune. Previously, gentility had ruled out the full development of her potential. Her first writings popularized economic and political issues by presenting them as everyday human concerns. In time, the outspoken, prolific writer would become a Victorian household name. Her importance went beyond popularization of difficult issues; she helped shape nineteenth-century intellectual life in a patriarchal society.

Martineau transformed travel writing, which had been not much more than entertainment, into social science. She believed—and illustrated—that as a woman she was actually in a better position than a man to research and blend sociology, anthropology, and political science. Furthermore, as evident in the following passage, she maintained that the ideal traveler should not begin from a position of prejudice and superiority, as so many contemporary British travel writers did. Rather, Martineau—who was an outspoken abolitionist, feminist, and Unitarian—approached the South with sympathy and cultural sensitivity. Accompanied by Louisa Jeffreys, she systematically explored and analyzed American society. She met leading American political figures, including Henry Clay, Daniel Webster, John Marshall, and Andrew Jackson. Her approach was to compare and contrast the reality of Jacksonian America with the ideals expressed in the Declaration of Independence and the Constitution. Although she disagreed with American positions on many major issues, she concluded positively that the United States was developing an egalitarian society.

Unlike many travel writers of the time, she was not repulsed by the difficulties of travel in America or Americans' relatively crude manners. More importantly she believed that her observations demanded analysis tempered by time and distance. Her approach to her travels gave her even more popularity and credibility than her previous writing had. Consequently, she was a major figure in informing the British reading public about events preceding the American Civil War. More importantly, early in the Civil War, when Great Britain could have recognized the Confederacy, Martineau, the eminent writer and humanitarian, was in a position to keep the slavery issue at the center of the debate.

Harriet Martineau, *Society in America*. 2 vols. (New York: Saunders and Otley, 1837), I: 219–231.

We had bespoken accommodations for the night at the hotel at Montgomery, by a friend who had preceded us. On our arrival at past eleven o'clock, we found we were expected; but no one would have guessed it. In my chamber, there was neither water, nor sheets, nor anything that afforded a prospect of my getting to rest, wet as my clothes were. We were hungry, and tired, and cold; and there was no one to help us but a slave, who set about her work as slaves do. We ate some biscuits that we had with us, and gave orders, and made requests with so much success as to have the room in tolerable order by an hour after midnight. When I awoke in the morning, the first thing I saw was, that two mice were running after one another round my trunk, and that the floor of the room seemed to contain the dust of a twelvemonth. The breakfast was to atone for all. The hostess and another lady, three children, and an array of slaves, placed themselves so as to see us eat our breakfast; but it seemed to me that the contents of the table were more wonderful to look at than ourselves. Besides the tea and coffee, there were corn bread, buns, buck-wheat cakes, broiled chicken, bacon, eggs, rice, hominy, fish, fresh and pickled, and beef-steak.

The hostess strove to make us feel at home, and recommended her plentiful meal by her hearty welcome to it. She was anxious to explain that her house was soon to be in better order. Her husband was going to Mobile to buy furniture; and, just now, all was in confusion, from her head slave having swallowed a fish bone, and being unable to look after the affairs of the house. When our friends came to carry us to their plantation, she sent in refreshments, and made herself one of the party, in all heartiness.

It was Sunday, and we went to the Methodist church, hoping to hear the regular pastor, who is a highly-esteemed preacher. But a stranger was in the pulpit, who gave us an extraordinary piece of doctrine, propounded with all possible vehemence. His text was the passage about the tower of Siloam; and his doctrine was that great sinners would somehow die a violent death. Perhaps this might be thought a useful proposition in a town where life is held so cheap as in Montgomery; but we could not exactly understand how it was derived from the text. The place was intensely light and hot, there being no blinds to the windows, on each side of the pulpit: and the quietness of the children was not to be boasted of.

On the way to our friends' plantation, we passed a party of negroes, enjoying their Sunday drive. They never appear better than on such occasions, as they all ride and drive well, and are very gallant to their ladies. We passed a small prairie, the first we had seen; and very serene and pretty it looked, after the forest. It was green and undulating, with a fringe of trees.

Our friends, now residing seven miles from Montgomery, were from South Carolina; and the lady, at least, does not relish living in Alabama. It was delightful to me to be a guest in such an abode as theirs. They were about to build a good house: meantime, they were in one which I liked exceedingly: a log-house, with the usual open passage in the middle. Roses and honeysuckles, to which humming-birds resort, grew before the door. Abundance of books, and handsome furniture and plate, were within the house, while daylight was to be seen through its walls. In my well furnished chamber, I could see the stars through the chinks between the logs. During the summer, I should be sorry to change this primitive kind of abode for a better.

It is not difficult to procure the necessaries and comforts of life. Most articles of food are provided on the plantation. Wine and groceries are obtained from Mobile or New Orleans; and clothing and furniture from the north. Tea is twenty shillings English per lb.; brown sugar, threepence-half penny; white sugar, sixpence-halfpenny. A gentleman's family, where there are children to be educated, cannot live for less than from seven hundred pounds to one thousand pounds per annum. The sons take land and buy slaves very early; and the daughters marry almost in childhood; so that education is less thought of, and sooner ended, than in almost any part of the world. The pioneers of civilisation, as the settlers in these new districts may be regarded, care for other things more than for education; or they would not come. They are, from whatever motive, money-getters; and few but money-getting qualifications are to be looked for in them. It was partly amusing, and partly sad, to observe the young people of these regions; some, fit for a better mode of life, discontented; some youths pedantic, some maidens romantic, to a degree which makes the stranger almost doubt the reality of the scenes and personages before his eyes. The few better educated who come to get money, see the absurdity, and feel the wearisomeness of this kind of literary cultivation; but the being in such society is the tax they must pay for making haste to be rich.

I heard in Montgomery of a wealthy old planter in the neighbourhood, who has amassed millions of dollars, while his children can scarcely write their names. Becoming aware of their deficiencies, as the place began to be peopled from the eastward, he sent a son of sixteen to school, and a younger one to college; but they proved "such gawks," that they were unable to learn, or even to remain in the society of others who were learning; and their old father has bought land in Missouri, whither he was about to take his children, to remove them from the contempt of their neighbours. They are doomed to the lowest office of social beings; to be the mechanical, unintelligent pioneers of man in the wilderness. Surely such a warning as this should strike awe into the whole region, lest they should also perish to all the best purposes of life, by getting to consider money, not as a means, but an end.

I suppose there must be such pioneers; but the result is a society which it is a punishment to its best members to live in. There is pedantry in those who read; prejudice in those who do not; coxcombry among the young gentlemen; bad manners among the young ladies; and an absence of all reference to the higher, the real objects of life. When to all this is added that tremendous curse, the possession of irresponsible power, (over slaves,) it is easy to see how character must become, in such regions, what it was described to me on the spot, "composed of the chivalric elements, badly combined": and the wise will feel that, though a man *may* save his soul anywhere, it is better to live on bread and water where existence is most idealized, than to grow suddenly rich in the gorgeous regions where mind is corrupted or starved amidst the luxuriance of nature. The hard-working settler of the north-west, who hews his way into independence with his own hands, is, or may be, exempt from the curse of this mental corruption or starvation; but it falls inevitably and heavily upon those who fatten upon the bounty of Nature, in the society of money-getters like themselves, and through the labours of degraded fellow-men, whom they hold in their injurious power.

We saw several plantations while we were in this neighbourhood. Nothing can be richer than the soil of one to which we went, to take a lesson in cotton-growing. It will never want more than to have the cotton seed returned to it. We saw the plough, which is very shallow. Two throw up a ridge, which is wrought by hand into little mounds. After these are drilled, the seed is put in by hand. This plantation consists of nine hundred and fifty acres, and is flourishing in every way. The air is healthy, as the situation is high prairie land. The water is generally good; but, after rain, so impregnated with lime, as to be disagreeable to the smell and taste. Another grievance is, a weed which grows on the prairie, which the cows like in summer, but which makes the milk so disagreeable, that cream, half-an-inch thick, is thrown to the pigs. They only can estimate this evil who know what the refreshment of milk is in hot climates.

Another grievance is, that no trees can be allowed to grow near the house, for fear of the mosquitoes. Everything else is done for coolness; there are wide piazzas on both sides of the house; the rooms are lofty, and amply provided with green blinds; but all this does not compensate to the eye for the want of the shade of trees. The bareness of the villages of the south is very striking to the eye of a strange, as he approaches them. They lie scorching and glaring on the rising grounds, or on the plain, hazy with the heat, while the forest, with its myriads of trees, its depth of shade, is on the horizon. But the plague of mosquitoes is a sufficient warrant for any sacrifice of the pleasures of the eye; for they allow but little enjoyment of anything in their presence.

On this, and many other estates that we saw, the ladies make it their business to cut out all the clothes for the negroes. Many a fair pair of hands have I seen dyed with blue, and bearing the marks of the large scissars. The slave women cannot be taught, it is said, to cut out even their scanty and unshapely garments economically. Nothing can be more hideous than their working costume. There would be nothing to lose on the score of beauty, and probably much gained, if they could be permitted to clothe themselves. But it is universally said that they cannot learn. A few ladies keep a woman for this purpose, very naturally disliking the coarse employment.

We visited the negro quarter; a part of the estate which filled me with disgust, wherever I went. It is something between a haunt of monkeys and a dwelling-place of human beings. The natural good taste, so remarkable in free negroes, is here extinguished. Their small, dingy, untidy houses, their cribs, the children crouching round the fire, the animal deportment of the grown-up, the brutish chagrins and enjoyments of the old, were all loathsome. There was some relief in seeing the children playing in the sun, and sometimes fowls clucking and strutting round the houses; but otherwise, a walk through a lunatic asylum is far less painful than a visit to the slave quarter of an estate. The children are left, during working hours, in the charge of a woman; and they are bright, and brisk, and merry enough, for the season, however slow and stupid they may be destined to become.

My next visit was to a school—the Franklin Institute, in Montgomery, established by a gentleman who has bestowed unwearied pains on its organization, and to whose care it does great credit. On our approach, we saw five horses walking about the enclosure, and five saddles hung over the fence: a true sign that some of the pupils came from a distance. The school was hung with prints; there was a collection of shells; many books and maps; and some philosophical apparatus. The boys, and a few girls, were steadily employed over their books and mapping; and nothing could exceed the order and neatness of the place. If the event corresponds with the appearance, the proprietor must be one of the most useful citizens the place has yet been honoured with.

I spent some days at a plantation a few miles from Montgomery, and heard there of an old lady who treats her slaves in a way very unusual, but quite safe, as far as appears. She gives them knowledge, which is against the law; but the law leaves her in peace and quiet. She also commits to them the entire management of the estate, requiring only that they should make her comfortable, and letting them take the rest. There is an obligation by law to keep an overseer; to obviate insurrection. How she manages about this, I omitted to inquire: but all goes on well; the cultivation of the estate is creditable, and all parties are contented. This is only a temporary ease and contentment. The old lady must die; and her slaves will either be sold to a new owner, whose temper will be an accident; or, if freed, must leave the State: but the story is satisfactory in as far as it gives evidence of the trust-worthiness of the negroes.

Our drives about the plantation and neighbouring country were delicious. The inundations from the rivers are remarkable; a perfect Eden appears when they subside. At the landing place of this plantation, I saw a board nailed near the top of a lofty tree, and asked what it could be for. It was the high-water mark. The river, the Alabama, was now upwards of twenty feet higher than usual; and logs, corn-stalks, and green boughs were being carried down its rapid current, as often as we went to the shore. There were evidences of its having laid even houses under water; but, on its subsiding, it would be found to have left a deposit of two inches and a half of fine new soil on the fields on either side of its channel. I never stood on the banks of the southern rivers without being reminded of Daniell's Views in India and Ceylon; the water level, shadowy and still, and the thickets actually springing out of it, with dark-green recesses, with the relief of a slender white stem, or dangling creeper here and there. Some creepers rise like a ladder, straight from the water to a bough one hundred and twenty feet high. As for the softness of the evening light on the water, it is indescribable. It is as if the atmosphere were purified from all mortal breathings, it is so bright, and yet not dazzling; there is such a profusion of verdure.

There were black women ploughing in the field, with their ugly, scanty, dingy dresses, their walloping gait, and vacant countenance. There were scarlet and blue birds flitting over the dark fallows. There was persimon sprouting in the woods, and the young corn-plants in the field, with a handful of cotton-seed laid round each sprout. There was a view from a bluff which fully equalled all my expectations of what the scenery of the southern States would be; yet, tropical as it was in many respects, it reminded me strongly of the view from Richmond Hill. We were standing on the verge of a precipice, of a height which I dare not specify. A deep fissure to our right was spanned by a log which it made one shudder to think of crossing. Behind us lay a cotton-field of 7,000 acres within one fence. All this, and the young aloes, and wild vines, were little enough like Richmond; and so was the faint blue line of hills on the horizon; but it was the intervening plain, through which the river ran, and on which an infinite variety of noble trees grew, as it appeared, to an interminable distance. Here their tops seemed woven into compactness; there they were so sprinkled as to display the majesty and grace of their forms. I looked upon this as a glorification of the Richmond view.

It was now the middle of April. In the kitchen garden the peas were ripening, and the strawberries turning red, though the spring of 1835 was very backward. We had salads, young asparagus, and radishes.

The following may be considered a pretty fair account of the provision for a planter's table, at this season; and, except with regard to vegetables, I believe it does not vary much throughout the year. Breakfast at seven; hot wheat bread, generally sour; corn bread, biscuits, waffles, hominy, dozens of eggs, broiled ham, beef-steak or broiled fowl, tea and coffee. Lunch at eleven; cake and wine, or liqueur. Dinner at two; now and then soup (not good,) always roast turkey and ham; a boiled fowl here, a tongue there; a small piece of nondescript meat, which generally turns out to be pork disguised; hominy, rice, hot corn-bread, sweet potatoes; potatoes mashed with spice, very hot; salad and radishes, and an extraordinary variety of pickles. Of these, you are asked to eat everything with everything else. If you have turkey and ham on your plate, you are requested to add tongue, pork, hominy, and pickles. Then succeed pies of apple, squash, and pumpkin; custard, and a variety of preserves as extraordinary as the preceding pickles: pine-apple, peach, limes, ginger, guava jelly, cocoa-nut, and every sort of plums. These are almost all from the West-Indies. Dispersed about the table are shell almonds, raisins, hickory, and other nuts; and, to crown the whole, large blocks of ice-cream. Champagne is abundant, and cider frequent. Ale and porter may now and then be seen; but claret is the most common drink. During dinner a slave stands at a corner of the table, keeping off the flies by waving a large bunch of peacock's feathers fastened into a handle,—an ampler fan than those of our grandmothers.

Supper takes place at six, or seven. Sometimes the family sits round the table; but more commonly the tray is handed round, with plates which must be held in the lap. Then follow tea and coffee, waffles, biscuits, sliced ham or hung-beef, and sweet cake. Last of all, is the offer of cake and wine at nine or ten.

The profits of cotton-growing, when I was in Alabama, were thirty-five per cent. One planter whom I knew had bought fifteen thousand dollars' worth of land within two years, which he could then have sold for sixty-five thousand dollars. He expected to make, that season, fifty or sixty thousand dollars of his growing crop. It is certainly the place to become rich in; but the state of society is fearful. One of my hosts, a man of great good-nature, as he shows in the treatment of his slaves, and in his family relations, had been stabbed in the back in the reading-room of the town, two years before, and no prosecution was instituted. Another of my hosts carried loaded pistols for a fortnight, just before I arrived, knowing that he was lain in wait for by persons against whose illegal practices he had given information to a magistrate, whose carriage was therefore broken in pieces, and thrown into the river. A lawyer with whom we were in company one afternoon, was sent for to take the deposition of a dying man who had been sitting with his family in the shade, when he received three balls in the back from three men who took aim at him from behind trees. The tales of jail-breaking and rescue were numberless; and a lady of Montgomery told me that she had lived there four years, during which time no day, she believed, had passed without some one's life having been attempted, either by duelling or assassination. It will be understood that I describe this region as presenting an extreme case of the material advantages and moral evils of a new settlement, under the institution of slavery. The most prominent relief is the hospitality,—that virtue of young society. It is so remarkable, and to the stranger so grateful, that there is danger of its blinding him to the real state of affairs. In the drawing-room, the piazza, the barouche, all is so gay and friendly, there is such a prevailing hilarity and kindness, that it seems positively ungrateful and unjust to pronounce, even in one's own heart, that all this way of life is full of wrong and peril. Yet it is impossible to sit down to reflect, with every order of human beings filling an equal space before one's mental eye, without being struck to the soul with the conviction that the state of society, and no less of individual families, is false and hollow, whether their members are aware of it or not; that they forget that they must be just before they can be generous. The severity of this truth is much softened to sympathetic persons on the spot; but it returns with awful force when they look back upon it from afar.

In the slave quarter of a plantation hereabouts I saw a poor wretch who had run away three times, and been re-captured. The last time he was found in the woods, with both legs frost-bitten above the knees, so as to render amputation necessary. I passed by when he was sitting on the door-step of his hut, and longed to see him breathe his last. But he is a young man, likely to drag out his helpless and hopeless existence for many a dreary year. I dread to tell the rest; but such things must be told sometimes, to show to what a pass of fiendish cruelty the human spirit may be brought by merely witnessing the exercise of irresponsible power over the defenceless. I give the very words of the speaker, premising that she is not American by birth or education, nor yet English.

The master and mistress of this poor slave, with their children, had always treated him and his fellow-slaves very kindly. He made no complaint of them. It was not from their cruelty that he attempted to escape. His running away was therefore a mystery to the person to whom I have alluded. She recapitulated all the clothes that had been given to him; and all the indulgences, and forgivenesses for his ingratitude in running away from such a master, with which he had been blessed. She told me that she had advised his master and mistress to refuse him clothes, when he had torn his old ones with trying to make his way through the woods; but his master had been too kind, and had again covered his nakedness. She turned round upon me, and asked what could make the ungrateful wretch run away a third time from such a master?

"He wanted to be free."

"Free! from such a master!"

"From any master."

"The villain! I went to him when he had had his legs cut off, and I said to him, it serves you right . . ."

"What! when you knew he could not run away any more?"

"Yes, that I did; I said to him, you wretch! but for your master's sake I am glad it has happened to you. You deserve it, that you do. If I were your master I would let you die; I'd give you no help nor nursing. It serves you right; it is just what you deserve. It's fit that it should happen to you . . . !"

"You did not—you dared not so insult the miserable creature!" I cried.

"Oh, who knows," replied she, "but that the Lord may bless a word of grace in season!"

Some readers may conceive this to be a freak of idiotcy. It was not so. This person is shrewd and sensible in matters where rights and duties are not in question. Of these she is, as it appears, profoundly ignorant; in a state of superinduced darkness; but her character is that of a clever, and, with some, a profoundly religious woman. Happily, she has no slaves of her own: at least, no black ones.

I saw this day, driving a wagon, a man who is a schoolmaster, lawyer, almanack-maker, speculator in old iron, and dealer in eggs, in addition to a few other occupations. His must be a very active existence.

This little history of a portion of my southern journey may give an idea of what life is in the wilder districts of the south.

11

P. T. Barnum

February 1837

Phineas Taylor Barnum (1810–1891) was the prototypical American impresario. His genius to assess the American public mood began with his release from a sixty-day jail stint—the Universalist Barnum having been jailed for attacking those who wanted to unite church and state. Barnum was able to orchestrate his release as a public relations event. He never lost that skill.

After rather mundane beginnings, P. T. Barnum began his rise to immortality as America's greatest showman. The following passage illustrates his professional beginning. Within five years, he had acquired the American Museum in New York. Some of his exhibits, such as the Feejee Mermaid and the 161-year old nurse to George Washington, were outright hoaxes. He was, however, attempting to teach Americans to indulge in innocent amusements, rather than resort to intemperance and vice. As leisure time increased for the middle classes, Barnum offered the public harmless diversion; he taught Americans how to play. When he appeared in Montgomery for the first time in February 1837, Barnum's Grand Scientific and Musical Theatre featured only a few performers. When he returned in 1847, Barnam was famous, even in Europe. The marketing genius presented Chang and Eng, the original Siamese twins; General Tom Thumb, the midget; and Jenny Lind, the Swedish Nightingale. (She did not sing in Montgomery, but Montgomerians took steamboats down to Mobile to revel in her fame.) Still later, he organized the first three-ring circus, Barnum and Bailey Circus, "The Greatest Show on Earth," which eventually featured Jumbo, the giant African elephant.

Barnum's love of life, sense of humor, ability to spot a winning act, and understanding of American taste are evident in the passage below; these talents made him a very rich man, and they made Barnum himself the greatest exhibit he ever presented.

P. T. Barnum, *The Life of P. T. Barnum,* (New York: Redfield, 1855), 196–198.

We reached Montgomery, Ala., February 28th, 1837 [by way of the Federal Road from Columbus, Georgia]. Here we met a legerdemain performer by the name of Henry Hawley. He was about forty-five years of age, but being prematurely gray, he has the appearance of a venerable gentleman of seventy. He purchased one half of my exhibition.

Hawley has much ready wit—a happy way of localizing most of his tricks—was very popular in that part of the country, where he had been performing for several years—and I never saw him "nonplussed" but once. It was in the performance of the trick called "The Egg Bag and the Old Hen." It is done in the following manner:

The exhibitor has a bag in which he declares there is an old hen, that will lay as many eggs as he pleases. He turns the bag inside out. There is apparently nothing in it; but actually, between the outside of the bag and the lining, is a small pocket so contrived with divisions as to hold six eggs. Having convinced the audience that there is nothing in the bag, he commands the hen to lay, and produces an egg. This he does, showing the inside and outside of the bag, each time, until all are gone but one. Keeping his hand on that part of the bag which covered the last egg, he puts the rest of the bag on the ground, and stamps upon it, to show that there is no deception; then, stating that he can have as many more eggs as he pleases, pulls out the last. "Before I take any more out," he says, "I will satisfy you that the eggs are real." At this time he stands in front of his table, and while breaking upon a plate an egg which he holds in his right hand, the empty bag is in his left hand. All eyes are turned upon the egg to see whether it is genuine or not. While the exhibitor thus distracts the attention of the audience, he slily passes his left hand to the back of the table, and hangs his empty bag on a hook which is placed there. At the same instance he detaches from another hook, behind the table, a bag exactly similar to the one which held the eggs, but which bag contains a hen.

"Now," says the exhibitor, "having seen that the eggs are real, I will show you the old hen that laid them." Dropping the mouth of the bag upon the ground, he turns out the old hen, to the astonishment of the audience.

On the occasion to which I allude, we did not reach the town where we were to exhibit until two o'clock in the afternoon. We had advertised a performance for three o'clock, and the village was already swarming with country people who came "to see the show." We put up the canvas as soon as possible. Hawley arranged his table, and not having time to prepare his "old hen" trick, he handed the bag to a negro boy attached to the tavern where we stopped, told him to catch an old hen, and put her into the bag, and he should "see the show for nothing." The darkey soon returned, handed the bag to Hawley, and passed in.

The old hen was duly hung up at the back of the table, our fiddler played a tune, (we had but one musician yet,) the curtain rose, and old Hawley opened the performances. He first exhibited several dexterous tricks with cups and balls—swallowed apparently a pound of tow—blew fire from his mouth, and then drew many yards of various-colored ribbons from the same receptacle. These were followed by wonderful tricks with iron rings, strings, and keys; he apparently swallowed a watch, and pulled an unknown quantity of cabbages, turnips and onions from the bosom of a verdant young countryman who volunteered to "assist" at the performances.

Hawley then commenced the great trick of the day, producing egg after egg as if by magic. The audience applauded him to the echo. He felt they were with him, and with triumphant exultation he exclaimed, "And now I will show you the old hen that laid all the eggs." He emptied the bag, and a bird appeared—but, alas, it was a *rooster!* Everyone was thunderstruck at the phenomenon, but when the old cock, who was very indignant at his confinement, strutted across the stage, shook his ruffled feathers, and began to crow, as if in defiance—the whole audience burst into a shriek of laughter, and Hawley, confounded and abashed, bolted into the dressing-room, cursed the stupidity of the black "fowl-fancier," and threatened to break the rascal's head, at the same time declaring he would not again appear in front of the curtain. Nor did he. He might have turned the accident to good account, and he probably would have done so nine times out of ten, but the thing was so totally unexpected, and the audience had so fair a start in merriment before he could recover self-possession, that he was literally obliged to quit the field.

Contemporary lithograph of G. Endicott's Montgomery Hall hotel, which opened in the fall of 1837.

12

Louis Fitzgerald Tasistro

March 1841

Louis Fitzgerald Tasistro (1808–1868) came to the United States from Ireland as a young man. Although he played on the New York stage, he was not particularly successful, so he turned to the Southern stage where he did little better. His specialty was tragic Shakespearean roles. He lectured in the Northeast and, as evidenced in the following passage, in Montgomery. He served as a journalist for a Boston newspaper and he also published a novel, and, as a travel writer, the two-volume *Random Shots*. Before the Civil War, he worked as a translator for the U.S. State Department, as well as teaching languages in Washington. Later, he returned to the New York theater. By 1872, Tasistro was so ill and destitute that his friend Walt Whitman made a public appeal for his relief.

Random Shots has long digressions on a variety of subjects, but Tasistro does write interesting descriptive passages. His seriousness, however, is questionable. He certainly exhibits the Blarney of an Irishman.

Louis Fitzgerald Tasistro, *Random Shots and Southern Breezes*, 2 vols. (New York: Harper & Brothers, 1842), II: 81–83, 89, 90–91, 96–98, and 100–101.

On my arrival at Montgomery, I found that quiet and sober-minded town in an unusual state of excitement, owing to the late freshets which had inundated the State of Alabama, destroying the crops on a great number of plantations, sweeping off all the live-stock that was upon them, and carrying away bridges of the greatest strength and the largest dimensions. It was the most disastrous occurrence of the kind that had taken place within the memory of the oldest inhabitants. Every new account was fraught with information of the most appalling character, and the public mind was thus kept in a perpetual whirl of anxiety and suspense. Dead cattle, trees torn up by the roots, and fragments of house-hold furniture, were seen floating on every stream for hundreds of miles around: in short, the demon of devastation had desolated the country far and wide, and a general earthquake could scarcely have changed the face of Nature more completely. To me, this state of things was particularly distressing; for, as the roads had been partially destroyed by the flood, so as to put an end to all travelling for several days, I had no alternative but to remain where I was: a circumstance which annoyed me excessively, as I had promised Mr. Abbott, the talented manager of the Charleston Theatre, to be in that city on a certain day.

I remember a very singular, though somewhat irreverent remark, made once in my presence by a wag, who, on being asked his opinion respecting a certain village, situated in one of the most retired and unobtrusive spots in the country, quaintly replied, that, little as he should like to live in such a place, he would be still more averse to dying there, for fear that he might be forgotten at the resurrection. Now, in my opinion, Montgomery is just such another place: still, I had no great reason, after all, to regret the circumstances which detained me there for a few days. An utter foe to indolence, and never more happy than when I am engaged either in acquiring or imparting information, I at once announced my intention of giving lectures, which was received with demonstrations of friendly feeling by nearly every intelligent person in the town. The public press seconded my efforts in the most liberal and obliging manner; while a clergyman of the Anabaptist persuasion tendered me the free use of his church, which, for excellence of sound, I found superior to any building I had ever before lectured in. It is not unworthy of remark, that in this place, so remote from the bustle and turmoil of the artificial world, I found an audience much more attentive and well-behaved than usually falls to the lot of a public speaker, even in those cities where refinement and politeness are supposed to have their headquarters.*

One advantage which I derived from this untoward delay was, that

* According to [source], Tasistro did, in fact, lecture on Shakespeare while in Montgomery.

it enabled me to take a dip into the circulating library of the town, and to familiarize myself, more than I had for some time been able to do, with what had been going on in the world of letters. After scrutinizing a dozen volumes or more of heterogeneous matter, without feeling very decidedly elevated by the operation, I took possession of Cooper's new novel of "Mercedes," with which I retired to the solitude of my chamber, pretty much in the spirit of the miser when he pays a periodical visit to his long-hoarded gold. The reiterated volleys of abuse which were about this time being poured upon this great and original writer, made me the more anxious to read this last production of his pen with all the attention due to a work coming from so distinguished a source. "Mercedes" has been condemned by the Whig press throughout the country in terms of absolute ferocity: by the other party it has been praised as at least equal to any of Mr. Cooper's previous productions.

[Five pages of Tasistro's analysis of James Fenimore Cooper's *Mercedes of Castile* is omitted.]

CHAPTER XX.

After a week's vegetation in the peaceful town of Montgomery, and just as I was beginning to forget all that lay beyond its quiet precincts, I was suddenly roused into action, one morning, by the unexpected intelligence that an extra coach would be started expressly for my accommodation, and that of sundry letter bags that had been waiting, like myself, with exemplary patience, for a chance to proceed on their journey. It is true that the "regular line" had been running for the last three days, or since the abatement of the flood; but so great was the number of passengers who had been detained, like myself, by the breaking up of the roads, and whose names had been registered in advance of mine, that at every departure I had been left behind. The immense quantity of luggage with which I was encumbered had very nearly proved an insurmountable obstacle to my ever proceeding farther; and it was only by paying double fare through Alabama and Georgia that I was permitted to get on at all.

. . . My tète-à-tète with the mail-bags was not quite as un-interesting as the sapient reader may imagine, although, to say the truth, I wish they had been sewed a little tighter, as it is not, to my notion, the pleasantest thing in the world to be alone in a mail-coach, with letter-bags before one, ripped open in various places, as was the case in this instance. But oh! what scope for reflection the sight of those bags afforded me! what a theme for the imagination to luxuriate upon! what a world of human interests lay hid in those silent messengers of fate! I actually felt myself growing too big for the coach, as, through the mist of fancy, I contemplated the multitude of agonized minds and panting hearts which the contents of those mysterious bags would tranquillize, or relieve, or lacerate! from the tender epistle, breathing forth, in accents of exquisite pathos, the first acknowledgments of love—the mournful sheet, with its black border, going forth on its errand of wo—the politician's address, pregnant with schemes for self-aggrandizement—the mandate of the man in power, fraught with the ruin or consummation of human hopes—the inexorable creditor's appeal, and the attorney's bill of costs—down to the rejected article, which will plunge some starving author into the very depths of despair: all, all of these, and myriads of others, rose before my bewildered fancy like ghosts conjured from the dark recesses of the earth by the wizard's wand. The greater portion, however, of the contents of these bags consisted of newspapers, showing the widespread popularity of that species of *literature,* and the insatiable thirst for information everywhere felt and manifested, from the heart of the gay city to the most solitary cottage in the wilderness. On this subject I may be permitted to make a few remarks.

. . . All ordinary modes of expression would fail to describe the state of the roads after we left Montgomery. In many places, indeed, there was no road at all; every trace of it had been obliterated, and our driver had occasion to call all his skill in navigation into play in order to guide the coach with any tolerable degree of safety. I could hardly have believed it possible for such wide-spread devastation to have been effected in so short a time. In whatever direction the eye was turned, it was sure to encounter traces of the havoc that had been made; and where the ground was hilly, and, consequently, more affected by the action of the water, the sweeping torrent had worn cavities so deep, that, as the carriage passed over the narrow and dangerous paths formed in the sides of the ridges, one could not help shuddering at the danger of being upset in such places—a fate, too, which seemed scarcely avoidable. This was but child's play, however, compared with the nervous excitement occasioned by crossing large pools of water every ten minutes, and frequently when the height of the flood had rendered the ordinary method of fording impracticable. To be waked up in the middle of a dark, starless night, and desired to walk over a slippery log of wood carelessly thrown across a boiling stream, as the passengers of the "regular line" were frequently called upon to do, might be considered excellent sport by some persons, but, for my own part, I must candidly confess that I never could perceive the least imaginable degree of pleasure in it. Accordingly, whenever the signal was given for that horrible experiment to be made, I always adhered immoveably to the inside of my "extra;" and when I heard a splash in the water, and the loud cachinnation which followed it—infallible indications that some "moving accident—by flood," not "field"—had befallen the adventurous pedestrians—I congratulated myself upon my pertinacity in preferring the remote chance of a broken neck to the more immediate prospect of a sound ducking. I had many alarms, but no positive catastrophe.

Well, after all, I like stagecoaches and stagecoach travelling, provided the first be moderately respectable, and the latter only moderately continued: one hears of life and sees character. The inside of a stagecoach is the high place of selfishness or of real inbred politeness; the stagecoach breakfast or dinner is a marvellous revealer of secrets, touching temper and disposition; and if you change your passengers often, and find out the subjects on which they are best informed, you may, in a short journey, pick up the history of half a state, or, at least, make yourself acquainted with its opinions. The most instructive and entertaining companions are not always those the most genteel: such so denominated *par excellence* are extremely apt to be sulky; or, having led as conventional a life as yourself, have as little free, fresh, racy character—you talk over the gay world, but you learn nothing of the country through which you are travelling. I love plain, homely, and, withal, respectable passengers; such as presume you to be interested in, and not altogether unacquainted with, the subjects most familiar to themselves . . .

. . . After a ride of seven hours through one of the wildest countries that the hand of civilization ever had to deal with in making a road, we stopped at a most unpromising-looking edifice, in the midst of the wilderness, where we found, nevertheless, an abundant supply of those choice delicacies, so peculiar to the backwoods, ylceped [called] ham and eggs, graphically spread out on a table of considerable length, evincing a degree of foresightedness on the part of mine host that was laudable in the extreme. Learning that the two coaches would make a halt of at least an hour, I paid my respects in a hasty manner to the aforesaid viands, advised the coachman of my intention to go on ahead on foot, and started accordingly, too happy of an opportunity to escape, even for so short a time, from the confinement I had hitherto been obliged to undergo. How much is lost of nature's grandeur and loveliness to him who catches but a passing view of either as he hurries along in a stagecoach—leaving railroad cars, from which absolutely nothing is seen, out of the question. The beauties of Nature are to be appreciated only by him who courts companionship with her—who pauses to watch her varying lights and shades—to gaze on the wild flower that gems her verdant robe—to listen to her voice, making melody among the leaves—and linking some charm of association or of sentiment with the different objects around him. It was on this occasion that I met one of those wild adventures, which, though attended with much inconvenience and no small danger at the time of their occurrence, afford such delightful materials for retrospection.

The road at this point was unusually free from mud, considering the abundance of swamps in this part of the country; and, except in the immediate vicinity of pools (of which there was no scarcity), the ground was dry, and afforded a pleasant walk . . .

[Tasistro continues on for many pages with a fastastical description of a colorful songbird which he saw and pursued until he was thoroughly lost, after which he spent the night in the woods and eventually miraculously stumbled upon the village where his stagecoach had stopped for the night. Thus reunited with his luggage and his companions, he sets out again and finally reaches Columbus, Georgia.]

13

George Lewis

April 1844

From his university days, **George Lewis** (1803–1879) identified with the evangelical wing of the Church of Scotland. He taught economics and edited a church-related newspaper before beginning his active ministry. When the Church of Scotland split in 1843, a third of the ministers and half the members left the established state church; Lewis took his congregation into the evangelical Free Church of Scotland. The new church, not having state support, immediately began raising funds elsewhere in Great Britain and in the North America. For six months in 1843–44, Lewis was part of a deputation that toured Canada and the United States to raise funds for the Free Church. Although this trip was financially successful, including raising monies from slave owners, his outspoken anti-slavery position caused controversy in the South. *Impressions of America* confirmed his spoken views. Furthermore, those who raised funds in slave-holding states were widely criticized—including by Frederick Douglass—and were encouraged to return the "blood-stained" donations and to break communion with churches in slave-holding states.

In Scotland, Lewis had long worked to alleviate the urban poverty and ignorance of industrial workers. Because of lack of success in this endeavor, Lewis eventually left his urban parish and abandoned his belief that British factory conditions could be improved by moral means. Subsequently, he retreated to a rural parish where he devoted his efforts to raising his five daughters.

Lewis was interested in the Presbyterian Church in America, as well as education, slavery, American labor conditions, and Scottish emigrants. Within these limits, Lewis's *Impressions of America* presents a very credible, informative account.

George Lewis, *Impressions of America and the American Churches: From Journal of the Rev. G. Lewis* (Edinburgh: W. P. Kennedy, 1845), 155–163.

I arrived in Montgomery, Alabama, about midnight on the 9th April, after three days and three nights staging, feverish and nervous from want of sleep and exercise, but found relief by the luxury of a bath and a sound sleep, and arose grateful to God for his protection over me throughout my journey. Inquiring for the Presbyterian minister, I found his carriage at the corner of the street. He received me cordially, and drove me for the night to his house, about a mile from the town. The prairies of Alabama begin but a little way out of the town—some woodland, others without any wood. Half a mile from his house, we came to one of the woodland prairies, where the sand ceases, and a rotten limestone, mixed with vegetable matter, forms a warm, rich, and very deep soil. The aspect and colour of the soil is very different from any I have lately passed through. Here there is a run of twenty miles of this fertile soil. Twenty years ago this land was sold at the State price of a dollar and a-half; now it is worth fifty dollars an acre.* The chief want in the prairies, in summer, is water; the surface wells all drying up. This has caused some of the wealthier settlers to form artesian wells, at the depth of some hundred feet, which they put down by augers or bores, about the diameter of your arm, and which at all seasons sends forth a stream of water, pure and cool. The wood of the Alabama prairies is all young and recent, having no appearance of antiquity. The trees are scattered over the meadow, forming ornaments rather than covers; and, by preserving the ground in some measure from the scorching sun, allow the rich pasture to spring up. Montgomery, as a town, is only twenty-five years old, having passed in that period from log-houses to frame-houses, and from frame-houses to brick, and now numbers 4,000 inhabitants.

The State of Alabama is 317 miles long, and 174 broad, containing about 28,160,000 acres. It lies between 30 and 35 degrees of north latitude, having the Gulf of Mexico and the Floridas on the south—Georgia on the east—the State of Tennesee on the north, and Mississippi on the west. The population has increased since 1810 as follows:—

* Roughly equivalent to $37 and $1,232, respectively, in today's currency.

1810	10,000
1814	29,683
1818	70,544
1820	127,901
1827	244,041
1830	308,997
1840	590,756

of this last number, 253,532 are slaves. The free coloured persons, male and female, are only 2,039. (Manummitted slaves cannot remain after manumission.) The rich prairies occupy the central part. The rest is rather hilly, and the banks of the rivers are said to be unhealthy. In 1840, the exports of this State amounted to nearly thirteen millions of dollars. It has three daily newspapers, and twenty-four weekly. The University of Alabama, which is liberally endowed by the State, I did not see. It is at Tuscaloosa, and was founded in 1820. In it, and Grange College, in the county of Franklin, the students do not exceed 152. The educational returns in 1840, give 114 academies, or grammar schools, with 5,018 scholars and 639 primary or common schools, with 16,243 scholars, which gives a *twenty-third* of the population at school, including the coloured people, or about a *twelfth* part, excluding those whom this State jealously exclude from the benefits of education, lest it should endanger their property and power over their fellow-men. The educational returns report not less than 22,592 persons, above twenty years of age, unable to read or write. This, no doubt, is the lowest, and not the highest number, indicating a very low state of education amongst the white population, compared with the northern or eastern States.

The Baptists report that they have in Alabama 250 churches; but, as they have only 109 ministers, these churches must be mere preaching stations. They have 11,445 communicants or members, which gives 105 members to each minister, or forty-five to each congregation. The Methodists have sixty ministers, and 13,845 members, or 231 members to each minister. The Presbyterians, twenty-five churches, and twenty-nine ministers, and 2,268 members, most of their churches being as yet only stations for preaching. The Roman Catholics have a bishop and five priests, and the Episcopalians seven ministers, but I could not learn the state of their congregations.

Every thing in this State is in its infancy, and it were a healthy promising infancy but for slavery. Even here railways are to be found. The Alabama and Florida railway extends from Pentacola, 156½ miles, to Montgomery and cost 2,500,000 dollars, and has a branch extending ten miles, from Selma to Cahawba. Most of this State was originally included in the territory of Georgia; but Georgia ceded her rights, and it was admitted into the Union in 1820 [1819].

The residence of the Presbyterian minister of Montgomery is not unlike a Scottish manse and glebe. House and grounds are, however, his own purchase, which he obtained, house and seventeen acres of the finest land, surrounded by a grove, for 1,500 dollars, about £300. Both he and his lady are from the neighbouring State of Georgia. His congregation is small, only eighty members, 250 sitters. The ladies of the congregation are at present working hard to erect a new church, and have got 1,000 dollars gathered by fancy fairs and suppers, at which they preside—thus drawing the world to help the church, means to which the church would never need to resort, if each of its members felt more the duty and privilege of aiding the cause of Christ with their substance. Let not those blame the Church for resorting to these arts, who, when applied to for aid, contribute a less sum to the cause of Christ than they spend weekly upon their meanest pleasures.

We had got into a pleasant conversation upon Scotland, and America, and Presbyterianism, &c., when the minister's only child would not take its tea, and began to look a little flushed. A mother's fears interpreted the symptoms into the beginning of scarlet fever. I ventured to hint that the child might have eaten too much, and that it should be suffered quietly to sleep it over, as it seemed quite disposed to do; but no! the little fellow must take his tea, which, with a full soul, he would have loathed, though it had been honeycomb—and so we had a scene, or succession of scenes. The child screamed itself into a fever, and I quite lost favour in the eyes of the lady by advocating the let-alone system, that nature might get time to work herself right. Scotland, America, and Presbyterianism were all forgotten, and I was quickly despatched to bed. In the morning the signs of scarlet fever, and every other kind of fever but the hunger fever, were gone. The lady had recovered her good humour. She said with a good humoured smile, "We loved so to talk about the Kirk." "It is *our sick child,*" said I.

On leaving Montgomery, we drove past the Town-house, in front of which was seated a band of young negroes and negresses, all under twenty years of age. There were not fewer than fifty, the one half females, sitting on one side, and the young men on the other. They looked so neat and clean, and their clothes so new and shining, that my first thought was that they were charity children dressed for some holiday scene. "What's this?" I exclaimed. "I am ashamed to say that is our slave market," was the reply. "They are decked out to attract customers." None of them was chained. They sat silent and demure—too silent and demure for holiday children. The salesman sat in the middle, rocking on a chair, balanced on its hind feet, his heels thrown upwards against a railing, and a newspaper in his hand. No one seemed at the time inquiring their price, but it was early, ere business had well begun. Such public exhibitions are still very common here, though no longer permitted in the Carolinas. I asked if they were field labourers, or domestic slaves, and learned that they were all field labourers. Their present dress is only for days of sale, and has been worn by many hundred young men and women in succession, who have gone through the same exhibition, like any other live stock tricked out for the market. As soon as sold, they are stripped of their ornaments, and reduced to their every day rags. We soon saw the truth of this in the appearance of a family of field labourers just dropped from a waggon, and standing in the streets half naked, whose single ragged garment of linen could hardly be detected to have been once of a white colour. That the law does occasionally, in this State, afford some protection to the poor slave in extreme cases, I am glad to learn. A planter in this neighbourhood was fined 10,000 dollars, some short time ago, for starving his slaves.

The household slaves I saw seemed to be lazy, and unserviceable. They did not come at the call of their mistress or master, took their own time, and were averse to any kind of work, out of the ordinary routine. The State of Alabama, by forbidding the manumitted slave to remain in the State in which he has been born and bred, and where all his earthly affections and interests are centred, has extinguished all hope and desire in the breast

Newspaper illustration of "Slave Auction in Montgomery, Alabama."

of the coloured population to better their condition, by services, however faithful and prolonged. The same act by which they have rivetted the chain, has rendered the slave a worse servant, and lowered his value to his master as a bondsman. As well destroy the mainspring of our watches, and expect the hands to point the right time, as take away *hope* and expect faithful service from human beings. If a manumitted slave is found in the State, he is sold for the *benefit of the State.* Thus does the tyrant majority act towards the minority, whose temporal destiny is in their hands, expecting to gather where they have not strawed, and by degrading their labourers, degrading themselves and their children, and retarding the permanent prosperity of their country, for the sake of their immediate interests, and to allay their present fears. Slave labour is only profitable when cotton is high priced. The fall of cotton, by the opening of new markets, would render slave labour more and more unprofitable, and make more obvious the impolicy as well as the inhumanity of slavery, in its *immediate* effects on their interests. The cultivation of cotton, like that of", is individual wealth and general poverty. Herds and flocks, and grain crops, are all forgotten in the growth of cotton or sugar; even, as in South America, no one thought of the greater riches to be procured from the surface of the soil, while anything was to be got by searching for the precious metals in the bowels of the earth. The low price of cotton in Alabama, while it would impoverish many of the present planters, and deprive them of their large returns for a few years, would ultimately enrich the country by an increased production of all the grains and fruits by which a nation multiplies those internal resources which no changes in commerce or in prices can permanently affect.

CHAPTER VII.

. . . We found a steamer from Montgomery to Mobile on the 12th April. The River Alabama, on which we sail, exhibits at the landing place the character of its floods. The river is no more than 100 feet below the banks, which it has excavated and hollowed out by its violence. The last year's flood has made serious inroads upon the foundations of a vast cotton store, which probably next flood will wholly undermine. At present the river is almost too low to admit of steam navigation, and this is amongst the last trips for the season from Montgomery to Mobile. The steamer is a long slender vessel, having a vast saloon running along its centre, divided into two compartments—that nearest the bow for the gentlemen, also used for dining, and that nearest the stern, being the remotest from the engine, for the ladies, who remain apart throughout the voyage, unless at meals, when they occupy the upper seats, not mingled with, but separated from the gentlemen, who sit lower down, unless they have ladies under their protection, when they sit next them, if they so choose, which they seldom, however, appear to do. The sleeping berths run along each side of this great saloon, and have two doors, one entering from the saloon, and the other from the open air; and by this management, whenever the vessel is in motion, a current of air is supplied by the two doors when open in whole or in part. Meanwhile you are safely secured in a recess from the current, which keeps the apartment sweet and comfortable in hot weather, without exposing you to its full draught. Nothing can be better contrived for this climate than these berths with their double doors. These vessels are very slightly built, and last only four or five years, but will sometimes pay in a single season.

14

Charles Lyell

January 1846

Charles Lyell (1797–1875), although born to privilege, earned his place as one of the most eminent men of science in the nineteenth century. After Oxford, he studied for the law and was admitted to the bar. His true interest, however, was geology, which he had first studied as a boy on his family's estates in the south of England and in Scotland before attending lectures at Oxford given by prominent scientists. Consequently, he left the law and devoted his professional life to science, especially to geology. His *Principles of Geology*, which was first published in three volumes in 1830 and which had eleven editions in Lyell's lifetime, first established his scientific credentials. He was a mentor of Charles Darwin, subscribed to a belief in evolution, but had difficulty accepting natural selection as the force behind evolution. In time, Lyell left the liberal wing of the Church of England for Unitarianism.

Lyell visited the United States four times, where he was received as one of the most famous and influential scientists of his day. He lectured to American audiences of up to three thousand. Therefore, when he visited Montgomery in 1846, he was already famous; two years later he was knighted.

He planned his trips with great care. His steady temperament, accurate observations, and the luxury of checking his judgment against his wife's enabled Lyell to produce one of the best accounts of mid-nineteenth century America, although he had not initially intended to publish his travel accounts. His interests in the South focused on geology and soil erosion, but also on public opinion, morals, and manners. His view on slavery was not so harsh as most of his non-Southern contemporaries; in fact, he compared Southern slaves with Northern free blacks. For this view, he was criticized by anti-slavery spokesmen, such as Frederick Douglas, who believed Lyell was too influenced by his slave-holding hosts.

Sir Charles served as a scientific adviser to the British government and worked with Prince Albert on the Crystal Palace exhibition of 1851. He was elected a member of the Royal Society, and he received the Geological Society's highest award. In 1864, he was made a baronet. Also indicative of his prominence is the fact that he was buried in Westminster Abbey. Today a mountain in Tasmania bears his name, as does a crater on the moon and another on Mars.

Charles Lyell, *A Second Visit to the United States of North America*, 2 vols. (London; John Murray, 1849), II: 41–44.

We at length arrived at Montgomery [by stage from Columbus to Chehaw and thence by rail], on the river Alabama, where I staid a few days to examine the geology of the neighbourhood. From the high ground near the town there is a distant view of the hills of the granitic region around Wetumpka. But the banks of the river at Montgomery are composed of enormous beds of unconsolidated gravel, thirty feet thick, alternating with red clay and sand, which I at first supposed to be tertiary, from their resemblance to strata near Macon and Augusta in Georgia. The fossil shells, however, of the accompanying marls (*Inoceramus* and *Rostellaria arenarum*), soon convinced me that they belonged to the cretaceous formation. About three miles south of the town there is a broad zone of calcareous marl, constituting what is called a prairie, or cane-brake country, bare of natural wood, and where there is so great a want of water, that it was at first difficult for settlers to establish themselves upon it, until, by aid of the Artesian auger, they obtained an abundant supply from a depth of 300, and often 500 feet, derived from the underlying gravelly and sandy beds. Farther from the outcrop of these gravelly beds borings have been made 800 feet deep without success. The temperature of the water was found to increase in proportion to the depth of the wells. A proprietor told me he had found it very difficult to get trees to grow on the prairie land, but he had succeeded, with great care, in rearing a few mulberries.

The common name for the marlite, of which this treeless soil is composed, is "rotten limestone." I found many lumps on the surface, much resembling white chalk, and containing shells of the genera, *Inoceramus, Baculite, Ammonite, Hippurite*, and that well-known fossil of the English chalk, *Ostrea vesicularis.*

In the market-place of Montgomery, I saw an auctioneer selling slaves, and calling out, as I passed, "Going for 300 dollars." The next day another auctioneer was selling horses in the same place. Nearly the same set of negroes, men, women, and boys, neatly dressed, were paraded there, day after day. I was glad to find that some settlers from the North, who had resided here many years, were annoyed at the publicity of this exhibition. Such traffic, they say, might as well be carried on quietly in a room. Another resident, who had come from Kentucky, was forming a party, who desire to introduce into Alabama a law, like one now in force in Kentucky, that no negroes shall henceforth be imported. By that statute, the increase of slaves has, he says, been checked. A case had lately occurred, of a dealer who tried to evade the law by bringing forty slaves into Kentucky, and narrowly escaped being fined 600 dollars for each, but has the ingenuity to get off by pretending that he was ignorant of the prohibition, and was merely passing through with them to Louisiana. "By allowing none to come in, while so many are emigrating to the West and Texas, we may hope," he said, "very soon to grow white."

Every evening, as nine o'clock, a great bell, or curfew, tolls in the market-place of Montgomery, after which no coloured man is permitted to be abroad without a pass. This custom, has, I understand, continued ever since some formidable insurrections, which happened many years ago, in Virginia and elsewhere. I was glad to find that the episcopal clergyman at Montgomery had just established a Sunday school for negroes. I also hear that a party in this church, already comprising a majority of the clergy, are desirous that the negro congregations should be represented in their triennial conventions, which would be an important step towards raising the black race to a footing of equality with the whites. In these times when many here are entertaining a hostile feeling towards Great Britain, and when the government is lending itself to the excitement, I find the ministers of the

Episcopal Church peculiarly free from such spirit, and cherishing a desire for peace and a friendly disposition towards the English. The Methodists had just been holding a protracted meeting in Montgomery, and such is the effect of sympathy and of the spirit of competition, that the religious excitement had spread to all the other sects.

. . . *Wednesday, Jan. 28.* 1846.—The steamer Amaranth was lying at the bluff at Montgomery on the Alabama river, and was advertised to sail for Mobile, a navigation of more than 300 miles, at ten o'clock in the morning.

15

Alexander Mackay

Summer 1846

Alexander Mackay (1808–1852), born in Scotland, began his journalism career in Canada; from Canada he traveled in the United States. Subsequently, he returned to Great Britain and worked for the *London Morning Chronicle*. In 1846, the newspaper sent him to the United States to report on the Oregon question. Mackay, who had a positive attitude about the United States, also reported on American government, commerce, manufacturing, agriculture, slavery, religion, and education. He was in the South from May to the early fall of 1846; his reports on the South were humorous, but unbiased. In fact, his volumes were among the most objective accounts of his time.

In 1847, he was called to the bar and soon left journalism for the law. His journalistic skills were again employed in 1851 when several British chambers of commerce sent him to India to report on cotton cultivation. He died at sea on his return voyage.

Alexander Mackay, *The Western World: or, Travels in the United States in 1846–47*, 2 vols. (Philadelphia: Lea and Blanchard, 1849), II: 65–66.

As a town, Montgomery is not calculated to leave so pleasing an impression upon the mind of the stranger as either Macon or Columbus. I stayed in it but an hour or two, during which I ascertained that it could offer very excellent accommodations to the traveller. After arriving I took the first steamer for Mobile, and found myself, in a little more than two hours after quitting the detestable stage-coach, steaming at the rate of eleven miles an hour down the winding channel of the Alabama.

Every step that we proceeded on our course to the Gulf served to develop more and more to the eye the inexhaustible resources of this noble State. Both sides of the river abounded with the evident signs of great fertility, and plantations on a scale equal to any in Georgia were passed in rapid succession. The country had not yet lost the picturesque and undulating aspect which it had assumed in western Georgia; whilst the vegetation with which the face of nature was clothed, and which was equally varied with, was if anything, still richer than that immediately to the east of the Chatahouchee. Montgomery is not at the head of steamboat navigation, the river being navigable for about forty miles further up to Wetumpka, where it is interrupted by the falls, and between which and Montgomery the country is so broken and varied as almost to deserve to have applied to it the epithet of rugged.

It was on the Alabama that I first found myself on board one of those high-pressure steamboats, which so often prove fatal to their passengers, and which have so ominous a name to European ears. It was some time ere I could reconcile myself to my position, and for most of the voyage I kept at a respectable distance from the boilers. We had but little cotton on board, although the boats on this river are sometimes very heavily laden with that commodity, on its way to Mobile for exportation, the quantity on board increasing at almost every station at which they call between Montgomery and that city.

As the voyage from Montgomery to the coast consumes at least the greater part of two days, the steamers on the Alabama are, of course, well provided with sleeping accommodations. The saloon, which extended almost from one end of the boat to the other, was lined on either side by a double row of excellent berths, in which the passengers could do anything except sleep. For this the berths were not to blame, the cause of it being the perpetual jarring of the boat, the powerful engines with which it was provided making it vibrate with every stoke, like a harp-string on being touched. There was a crowd of passengers on board, most of whom were, to judge from appearances, highly respectable; but there were a few whose look, conduct, and demeanour, but too plainly told to what class of desperadoes they belonged. They were most respectably dressed, but kept almost constantly together, there being too many people on board to allow of their carrying matters with the high hand with which they conduct their operations on the Mississippi and some of its tributaries. They belong to the class of professional gamblers, who form so large an ingredient in the population of the South; and, taking them altogether, they had the most sinister look about them that I had ever witnessed. It seemed to be generally understood who and what they were; and although a few conversed and played a little with them, they were prudently shunned by the great bulk of the passengers. Their gambling habits are not the only bad feature about them, it being sometimes their delight, and at other times their object, for reasons best known to themselves, to create disturbances amongst the passengers, which, in these fiery latitudes, are so often fatal to those who are implicated. When the voyage is long, and there are but few respectable people on board who can protect themselves by their numbers, a gang of these fellows are not only troublesome, but dangerous as fellow-passengers. Public opinion, however, is now, even in the South, so decidedly against them, that this great drawback to travelling in the South and West is fast diminishing.

"Burning of the Capitol of Alabama on December 14, 1849" with a view up Market Street (today's Dexter Avenue) from the artesian well. Philadelphian Stephen Decatur Button designed this Capitol; it served from 1847 until it burned in 1849. Two hotels are included: Madison House on the left and Montgomery Hall on the right. Sarony and Majors of New York made this lithograph from A. G. Parks's daguerreotype, which he took from the Court House steps.

16

Francis and Theresa Pulszky

April 1852

Ferencz Aurèl Pulszky (1814–1897) was born to privilege. His European travels resulted in a book on Great Britain, a country that he particularly admired, and that resulted in his membership in the Hungarian Academy. In 1848, Pulszky was elected to the Hungarian Reichstag; this was followed by government posts in both Budapest and Vienna. In short order, the Hungarian nationalist fled to England where he joined Lajos Kossuth, the Hungarian nationalist revolutionary leader. Together they and their wives traveled to the United States to raise support for the Hungarian cause. The South was not as supportive of the Hungarian cause as was the North, so the warm welcomes that Kossuth and Pulszky received in Mobile and Montgomery surprised them.

In 1852, Austria condemned Pulszky to death in absentia. Eight years later, he participated in the Italian unification movement, served with Garibaldi, and was imprisoned in Naples. After years in political exile, in 1866 he was amnestied by the Austrian emperor and returned to Budapest where he reentered political life. His contributions, however, were not limited to politics. He also served as an official of the Hungarian Academy and the director of the National Museum, as well as distinguishing himself as an archaeologist.

The diary that was the basis of *White, Red, Black* was actually kept by Pulszky's wife, Terézia Walder Pulszky (1819–1866). The book seriously addresses American slavery. Although the Pulszkys are critical, they are also objective. They observed a strong anti-black racism in the North and noted that few Southerners defended slavery, but that many wanted foreigners to understand the Southern slave system.

Francis and Theresa Pulszky, *White, Red, Black: Sketches of American Society in the United States*, 2 vols. (New York: Redfield, 1853), II: 114–119.

II. THE ALABAMA RIVER AND MONTGOMERY.

April 6th.—Amongst the shouts of the citizens of Mobile, we left on the 3d the hospitable city, which had greeted us with the warmest sympathy, the more unexpected to us, as one of the Senators of Alabama, Colonel Clemens, had made himself prominent in Washington City by his vehement invectives against Kossuth, though aware that his arguments had no more than six supporters in the Senate. We thought, therefore, that he had expressed the sentiments of his State, until the demonstration of the most important city in Alabama agreeably undeceived us.

We have scarcely yet made a more picturesque tour in the United States than the trip from Mobile to Montgomery, up the Alabama River. Here for the first time we felt ourselves amidst primitive nature, almost without any trace of culture. The river winds through a dense forest, unscathed by the fires of the Indians and by the axe of the settler. The pine, the black oak, and the cypress tower darkly over the lighter colored sycamores, poplars, elms and willows. Here and there we see a splendid magnolia or a magnificent live oak, adorned by festoons of Spanish moss. A venomous species of ivy, which causes inflammation if touched, curls up the trees; the white blossoms of the dogwood and the purple of the red-bud blend their color harmoniously with the glossy green of the laurel, which forms here the thick underwood. Patches of high-grown cane cover the little islands, and the Southern hue of the sky completes the delightful landscape. On long tracts no human abode meets the eye, distant smoke alone shows the presence of man; everything around is silent; on a falling withering tree rests a lazy tortoise; the kingfisher divides the air with bold strokes; dark butter-ducks, disturbed by the paddling of the steamer, flutter up in advance of the boat; while gulls bathe their breasts in the waves; swift pigeons flit over the woods; a host of cranes steer towards the north, and high in the air sails a lonely turkey-buzzard. The reddish clay of the soil is little fit for sugar or cotton, and no other crop repays slave-labor, the land is therefore left to its primitive freedom. Let the "Homestead Bill" pass, and the Alabama will bend its course through cornfields, and will team with steamers, whilst now we have met but one single boat in three days.

Yesterday afternoon we again saw plantations. The banks rose perpendiculary to about a hundred feet; the paths to the plantations were ladders: pulleys were used to let the cotton-bales down to the boats and to haul the cargo up. Numerous blacks and a few white men here gazed idly down on the river; it was Sunday, the day of rest. An old free negro, poorly clad, came down from one of the plantations and went along with us about twenty miles. When he reached the place to which he was going, he asked the purser for the price of his fare. He got the reply: "We do not charge such poor people as you." Our fellow-travellers were planters. All with whom we conversed, complained that Europeans did not understand the character of the "peculiar institution." "Were all the negroes free," said one of them, "they could not rise in their social position. In the presence of their former masters, impressed with the associations of their servitude, they always would only do menial work, they never would presume to consider themselves as equals to the white. There is a tendency amongst them to grow white in their posterity. A mulatto girl feels honored by marrying a lighter colored man; an alliance with a darker hue seems dishonorable to her. Therefore you will notice that the full blacks have become fewer in the course of time; in the cities you scarcely meet with any. One century has already made the great bulk of them lighter; in another century many of them will be assimilated to the whites."

Another gentleman remarked: "Had a large number of blacks in the last one hundred and fifty years been thrown on to the coasts of England, such as have been imported against our will into America, it is a great question whether, amidst the competition of a more energetic race, their number would not have dwindled down to insignificance. Surely they would be wretched paupers, inferior to our slaves, who are physically strong and morally better than any African tribe that has not passed through the school of slavery. Slavery has improved the race," he added.

A lady told me that her parents had come to the United States from Scotland when she was a little child; she had married a Southerner. After six of her daughters had married she and her husband took their seventh daughter to Europe, as the lady wished to visit her native country. "We went to Scotland," said she, "but everything was strange to me; I found all my relations dead, and people very ignorant about America. Once we met an Irish gentleman who had a son, a boy about twelve years old, who asked my daughter whether she was an American? He could not believe it, as she was fair, and he thought that all the Americans were black. My daughter told him that we had black servants in the houses and in the fields. 'What do you give them to eat?' asked the young Irish man. 'Why,' said she, 'what we eat ourselves, meat and vegetables every day.' The father of the boy seemed much astonished to hear it, and assured me that the poor people in Ireland who work in the fields taste meat but few times a year."

A gentleman of South Carolina asked me whether we had large farms in Hungary, and as he heard that estates of a thousand and even of ten thousand acres were not rare, he asked whether we had colored people to work them. He thought it remarkable that large tracts of land can be tilled for wages without compulsion. "In America," he said, "the great estates would all be broken up, had we no slaves. Were the blacks free, they would squat in the woods, they would easily earn enough to maintain their life, and no money could induce them to work for the planter. They have no higher wants, and therefore it is their greatest enjoyment to be idle. Moreover, white labor does not do for sugar or rice, and even for cotton in our hot climate, which only negroes can endure."

The evening was lovely; a gentle breeze slightly rippled the surface of the waters, and the shrill and wild strains of the negroes on board broke with peculiar charm the silence of the night. As often as we left the shore the blacks repeated a monotonous song which sounded like the wailing of a sad farewell.

When we came nearer to Montgomery the high cliffs on the banks disappeared. The river runs here through an undulating country; houses were scattered along the banks; a crowd was assembled along the landing-place, guns were fired, gentlemen displayed their horsemanship, carriages and committees awaited us, to take us to the city, but the shouting and cheering and the reports of the cannons frightened the horses, and I was

The 1851 Capitol, designed by Barachias Holt of Maine. This contemporary image was made from W. H. Freer's circa 1856 daguerreotype, which is one of the earliest images of the 1851 Capitol. Today this building is the central block of the Capitol, but it now has a south wing (1906), a north wing (1911), and a rear or east wing (1885 and 1992).

glad when we were safely lodged in the Exchange Hotel.

April 7th.—The charms of Southern nature adorn Montgomery, but the capitol of Alabama (which is thought to be the great feature of the city, with its high cupola covered with shining tin plate, with its Greek portico and two balconies behind the columns) looks more grotesque than fine. We made the acquaintance of an Americanized German, who took us to see all the attractions of the place. "What a nice house!" said I, observing a handsome cottage surrounded by a very elegantly cultivated garden. "It belongs to a gentleman who became bankrupt last fall; when he saw that his affairs were turning for the worse, he transferred his property to his wife."

"But that is dishonorable," objected I. "Why," said our companion, "it ceases to be so where it is a daily occurrence, and where the capitalists are prepared for it, and therefore do not lend their money under twenty per cent. I could show you several houses here which belong to the wives of ruined men. A bankrupt, if industrious, does not even lose his credit here; he can redeem it easily, for after his failure he is reckoned to be more experienced and more practical than before."

The German gentleman described to us the way in which people live and manage here. "Nobody," said he, "can do in these parts without slaves, though the occasional losses through them are sometimes very heavy. Last year, for instance, I bought a powerful fellow, and two weeks after he died. I rented him out to the road contractors, he got the ague in the swamps, and had I not insured his life before to the amount of one thousand dollars I should have lost my capital."

At the hotel, we met an amiable lady, the wife of a planter. In summer she resides in the North, in winter in Montgomery. She told me that her slaves on the plantation get up balls and dancing parties, and on such occasions use her plate, china and glass. "Our house-slaves," continued she, "are yet more under our immediate care. I often dress my maid when she goes to the ball; and when she was married, I adorned her with all my jewels. But the house-slaves likewise feel themselves the aristocrats among the colored people; they look down upon the field hands; they think them very vulgar and uncouth, and do not deign to greet them in the streets."

17

Fredrick Law Olmsted

March 1853

Frederick Law Olmsted (1822–1903), born in Connecticut, entered Yale College, but left after a semester. It was not formal education that made the man; rather it was travel—a year's voyage to China in his mid-teens, as well as three European visits—a six-month walking tour of Great Britain and months in Italy, Germany, and France. His observations resulted in newspaper articles, books, and a budding interest in landscape design, which would in time lead to his becoming the father of American landscape architecture.

In 1852, Olmsted made the first of two visits to the American South; in all, he spent a full year in the South. Sixty-four of his letters were published by the predecessor of today's *New York Times*. Subsequently, they were revised and published in three volumes, and even later as *The Cotton Kingdom*. His published works differ from the norm of travel writing on the antebellum South in that he did not merely report his observations with a few editorial comments, but he actually analyzed the South and found it wanting. Holding democratic ideals, Olmsted worked to elevate the North's popular culture. He believed that an improvement in Northern taste and morals would prove a free-labor society's superiority to a slave-labor society. His approach took several paths: editing *Putnam's Monthly Magazine*, which published work by Melville and Thoreau, as well an antislavery pieces. Olmsted also supported other antislavery publications, and raised funds to arm Kansas free soilers. Also, before the Civil War, Olmsted became the superintendent of New York City's Central Park—a naturalistic park that he and Calvert Vaux conceived and designed. He left this position at the beginning of the war to serve as chief executive officer of the U.S. Army's Sanitary Commission. This did not prove satisfactory, so Olmsted spent the last two years of the war in California dedicated to a variety of landscape projects, including designing the campus at Berkeley and San Francisco's public parks system, and serving as chairman of the Yosemite Valley Commission. At the end of the war, he returned to New York where he resumed work on the city's parks. Olmsted believed that not only the South and West required reinventing but so too did New York City, which was in need of civilization most of all.

Of the observers of the antebellum South, Olmsted ranks as one of the most astute, especially of the rural South and the yeoman farmers with whom he sympathized. He was ahead of his time to reject the idea of Southern white solidarity. During some of his travels by horseback, he had opportunities not available to those traveling by coach and steamboat. His personal observations were supplemented by wide reading, from government reports to local histories. A moderate man, he opposed slavery, but not to the extent that he wished to punish the South. Rather, he advocated gradual emancipation; in time, however, Olmsted became more critical of slavery, the general backwardness in the South, and the Southern elite. From a purely economic position, he calculated that a slave did approximately an eighth of the work of the best white laborer. In addition to slaves, he sympathized with poor Southern whites, who he judged to be lower than the lowest Northern classes, except those in the slums of New York City.

The following passage's confused chronology is the result of augmenting and transferring information from letters.

Frederick Law Olmsted, *A Journey in the Seaboard Slave States, with Remarks on Their Economy* (New York: Dix and Edwards, 1856), 549–565 and 574–577.

A day's journey took me from Columbus, through a hilly wilderness, with a few dreary villages, and many isolated cotton farms, with comfortless habitations for black and white upon them, to Montgomery, the capital of Alabama.

Montgomery is a prosperous town, with very pleasant suburbs, and a remarkably enterprising population, among which there is a considerable proportion of Northern and foreign-born business-men and mechanics.

I spent a week here very pleasantly, and then left for Mobile, on the steamboat Fashion, a clean and well-ordered boat, with polite and obliging officers. We were two days and a half making the passage, the boat stopping at almost every bluff and landing to take on cotton, until she had a freight of nineteen hundred bales, which was built up on the guards, seven or eight tiers in hight, and until it reached the hurricane deck. The boat was thus brought so deep that her guards were in the water, and the ripple of the river constantly washed over them. There are two hundred landings on the Alabama river, and three hundred on the Bigby (Tombeckbee of the geographers), at which the boats advertise to call, if required, for passengers or freight. This, of course, makes the passage exceedingly tedious.

The principal town at which we landed was Selma, a thriving and pleasant place, situated upon the most perfectly level natural plain I ever saw. In one corner of the town, while rambling on shore, I came upon a tall, ill-proportioned, broken-windowed brick barrack; it had no grounds about it, was close upon the highway, was in every way dirty, neglected, and forlorn in expression. I inquired what it was, and was informed, the "Young Ladies' College." There were a number of pretty private gardens in the town, in which I noticed several evergreen oaks, the first I had seen since leaving Savannah.

At Claiborne, another considerable village upon the river, we landed, at nine o'clock on a Sunday night. It is situated upon a bluff, a hundred and fifty feet high, with a nearly perpendicular bank, upon the river. The boat came to the shore at the foot of a plank slide-way, down which cotton was sent to it, from a warehouse at the top.

There was something truly Western in the direct, reckless way in which the boat was loaded. A strong gang-plank being placed at right angles to the slide-way, a bale of cotton was let slide from the top, and, coming down with fearful velocity, on striking the gang-plank, it would rebound up and out on to the boat, against a barricade of bales previously arranged to receive it. The moment it struck this barricade, it would be dashed at

Top: "Cotton-Shoot on the Alabama." Loading cotton onto the steamboat Magnolia on the Alabama River from the Illustrated London News*, 4 May 1861. This is the reverse image of the engraving printed in* Ballou's Pictorial Drawing-Room Companion*, 21 April 1855. The three-hundred-foot long shoot descends from the two-hundred-foot hill to the river. Above: "Foot of the Shoot: Receiving the Cotton-Bales on Board the Steamer." Loading cotton onto the steamboat Magnolia on the Alabama River from the* Illustrated London News*, 4 May 1861. The shoot is divided in half. On one side is the cotton shoot itself, and on the other are the steps.*

by two or three men, and jerked out of the way, and others would roll it to its place for the voyage, on the tiers aft. The mate, standing near the bottom of the slide, as soon as the men had removed one bale to what he thought a safe distance, would shout to those aloft, and down would come another. Not unfrequently, a bale would not strike fairly on its end, and would rebound off, diagonally, overboard; or would be thrown up with such force as to go over the barricade, breaking stanchions and railings, and scattering the passengers on the berth deck. Negro hands were sent to the top of the bank, to roll the bales to the side, and Irishmen were kept below to remove them, and stow them. On asking the mate (with some surmisings) the reason of this arrangement, he said "The niggers are worth too much to be risked here; if the Paddies are knocked overboard, or get their backs broke, nobody loses anything!"

The boat being detained the greater part of the night, and the bounding bales making too much noise to allow me to sleep, I ascended the bank by a flight of two hundred steps, placed by the side of the slide-way, and took a walk in the village. In the principal street, I came upon a group of seven negroes, talking in lively, pleasant tones: presently, one of them commenced to sing, and in a few moments all the others joined in, taking different parts, singing with great skill and taste—better than I ever heard a group of young men in a Northern village, without previous arrangement, but much as I have heard a strolling party of young soldiers, or a company of students, or apprentices, in the streets of a German town, at night. After concluding the song, which was of a sentimental character, and probably had been learned at a concert or theatre, in the village, they continued in conversation, till one of them began to whistle: in a few moments all joined in, taking several different parts, as before, and making a peculiarly plaintive music. Soon after this, they walked all together, singing, and talking soberly, by turns, slowly away. I allowed them to pass me, but kept near them, until they reached a cabin, in the outskirts of the village. Stopping near this a few minutes, two of them danced the "juba," while the rest whistled and applauded. After some further chat, one said to the rest: "Come, gentlemen, let's go in and see the ladies," opening the door of the cabin. They entered, and were received by three negro girls, with great heartiness; then all found seats on beds. and stools, and chests, around a great wood fire, and when I passed again, in a few minutes, they were again singing.

THE MUSICAL TALENT OF NEGROES.

The love of music which characterizes the negro, the readiness with which he acquires skill in the art, his power of memorizing and improvising music is most marked and constant. I think, also, that sweet musical voices are more common with the negro than with the white race—certainly than with the white race in America. I have frequently been startled by clear, bell-like tones, from a negro woman in conversation, while walking the streets of a Southern town, and have listened to them with a thrill of pleasure. A gentleman in Savannah told me that, in the morning after the performance of an opera in that city, he had heard more than one negro, who could in no way have heard it before, whistling the most difficult airs, with perfect accuracy. I have heard ladies say that, whenever they have obtained any new and choice music, almost as soon as they had learned it themselves, their servants would have caught the air, and they were likely to hear it whistled in the streets, the first night they were out. In all of the Southern cities, there are music bands, composed of negroes, often of great excellence. The military parades are usually accompanied by a negro brass band.

Dr. Cartwright, arguing that the negro is a race of inferior capabilities, says that the negro does not understand harmony; his songs are mere sounds, without sense or meaning. My observations are of but little value upon such a point, as I have had no musical education; but they would lead me to the contrary opinion. The common plantation-negroes, or deck-hands of the steamboats—whose minds are so little cultivated that they cannot count twenty—will often, in rolling cotton-bales, or carrying wood on board the boat, fall to singing, each taking a different part, and carrying it on with great spirit and independence, and in perfect harmony, as I never heard singers, who had not been considerably educated, at the North.

MATHEMATICAL CAPACITY.

Touching the intellectual capacity of negroes: I was dining with a gentleman, when he asked the waiter—a lad of eighteen—to tell him what the time was. The boy, after studying the clock, replied incorrectly; and the gentleman said it was impossible for him to make the simple calculation necessary. He had promised to give him a dollar, a year ago, whenever he could tell the time by the clock; had taken a good deal of trouble to teach him, but he did not seem to make any progress. I have since met with another negro boy, having the same remarkable inability—both the lads being intelligent, and learning easily in other respects: the first could read. I doubt if it is a general deficiency of the race; both these boys had marked depressions where phrenologists locate the organ of calculation.

A gentleman, whom I visited, in Montgomery, had a carpenter, who was remarkable for his mathematical capacities. Without having had any instruction, he was able to give very close and accurate estimates for the quantity of all descriptions of lumber, to be used in building a large and handsome dwelling, of the time to be employed upon it, and of its cost. He was an excellent workman; and, when not occupied with work directly for his master, obtained employment of others—making engagements, and taking contracts for jobs, without being required to consult his master. He had been purchased for two thousand dollars, and his ordinary wages were two dollars a day. He earned considerable money besides, for himself, by overwork at his trade, and still more in another way.

SLAVE HIGH LIFE.

He was a good violinist and dancer, and, two nights a week, taught a negro dancing-school, from which he received two dollars a night, which, of course, he spent for his own pleasure. During the winter, the negroes, in Montgomery, have their "assemblies," or dress balls, which are got up "regardless of expense," in very grand style. Tickets are advertised to these balls, "admitting one gentleman and two ladies, $1;" and "Ladies are assured that they may rely on the strictest order and propriety being observed." Cards of invitation, finely engraved with handsome vignettes, are sent, not only to the fashionable slaves, but to some of the more esteemed white people, who, however, take no part, except as lookers-on. All the fashionable dances are executed; no one is admitted, except in full dress: there are the regular masters of ceremonies, floor committees, etc.; and a grand supper always forms a part of the entertainment.

While in a book-store, in Montgomery, I saw a negro looking at some very showy London valentines. After examining the embossed envelopes, and the colored engravings of hearts and darts, and cupids and doves, he would ask the clerk to read the poetry, and listen while he did so, with the air of a profound critic. I heard ten dollars mentioned as the price of one of them; and I presume he was ready to pay that price, if he could find an adequate expression of his sentiment.

My friend had so much confidence in the discretion and faithfulness of his carpenter, that he seldom gave him any orders or directions. To enable him to execute some business with greater celerity, he, one day, in my observation, took a horse that his master was intending to use himself. When asked why he did so, he mentioned the object he had in view, and said: "I thought I needed him more than you did"—and was not reproved.

On visiting a piece of ground that his master owned, out of town, we found him engaged, with two black men and one white—a native, country fellow—in putting up a fence. The latter was acting under his orders; and, upon inquiry, I found that, seeing that the work was needed to be done immediately, he had hired him, as well as the two blacks, without consulting his master. It was the first case I had seen of a white man acting under the orders of a negro, though I have several times since seen Irishmen doing so.

This gay carpenter's wife was a woman of serious sentiments, and preferred prayer-meetings to balls; so they did not agree very well. She belonged to another gentleman, who did not live in the town, and was at service in another family than that with which her husband was connected. She had informed her owner that, if he would like to take her into the country with him, she had no particular objections to being separated from her husband. She did not like him very much—he was "so gay."

NATURAL AFFECTION OF NEGROES.

It is frequently remarked by Southerners, in palliation of the cruelty of separating relatives, that the affections of negroes for one another are very slight. I have been told by more than one lady that she was sure her nurse did not have half the affection for her own children that she did for her mistress's. But it is evident that this loyalty is not peculiar to the black race. Probably there are many white people in Europe, even in this day, who would let their children's lives be sacrificed to save the life of the son of their sovereign. They teach this as a duty, and use the Bible to make it appear so, in Prussia, if not in England.

A very excellent lady, to show me how little cruelty there was in the separation of husband and wife, told me that when she lived at home, on her father's plantation, in South Carolina, he had given her a girl for a dressing-maid. This girl, after a time, married a man on the plantation. The marriage ceremony was performed by an Episcopal clergyman, according to the prayer-book form—the parties, of course, promising to cleave together until death should part them. A year later, the lady herself was to be married, and was to remove with her husband to his residence in Alabama. She told the girl she could do as she pleased—go with her and leave her husband, or remain with her husband and be separated from her. She preferred to cleave to her mistress. She accordingly parted from her husband, with some expressions of regret for the necessity, but with no appearance of grief or sadness. Neither did the husband complain. A month after she reached her new residence in Alabama, she found a new husband; and it was supposed that her former husband had suited himself with a new woman. She had now been living ten years in Alabama, and had several children; she was expecting soon to be taken with her mistress on a visit to the old plantation in South Carolina, and laughed as she spoke of probably meeting her old husband again.

A slave, who was hired (not owned) by a friend of mine in Savannah, called upon him one morning while I was there, to say that he wished to marry a woman in the evening, and wanted a ticket from him to authorize the ceremony.

"I thought you were married," said my friend.

"Yes, master, but that woman hab leave me, and go 'long wid 'nodder man."

"Indeed! Why, you had several children by her, did not you?"

"Yes, master, we hab thirteen, but now she gone 'long wid 'nodder man."

"But will your church permit you to marry another woman so soon?"

"Yes, master; I tell 'em de woman I had leave me, and go 'long wid 'nodder man, and she say she don't mean to come back, and I can't be 'spected to lib widout any woman at all, so dey say dey grant me de divorce."

A pleasant example of the child-like confidence which a slave frequently has in his sovereign, when he is a good-hearted and trustworthy man, occurred to me at a hotel, where I had been waited upon for several days by an unusually good servant. One morning, while making a fire for me, he said—

"Dey say Congress is going to be bruck up in tree week— I'se glad enough o' dat."

"Glad of it—why so?"

"I'se got a master dah; I'll be a heap glad when he's come back."

"You want to see him again, eh?"

"Yes, sar. I won't stay long in dis place wen he com, nudder. I'll hab im get noder place for me. I don' like dis place, no how; dis place don' suit me; never saw sich a place. Dey keeps me up most all night; I haan been used to sich treatem. Dey haan got but one servant for all dis hall; dey ought to hab two at de least. I'm de olest servant in de house; all de odder ole servant is gone."

"And they have got Irishmen in their places."

"Yes! and what kine of servant is dey? Ha! all de Irish men dat ever I see haden so much sense in dar heds as I could carry in de palm of my han. I was de head waiter allers in my master's house till my brudder grew up, and I learned him; he's de head waiter now. And dis heah ant no kine of place for my sort; I don' stay here no longer wen my master come back."

A few mornings after this, he did not come into my room, as usual; I was out during the forenoon; when I returned, he came to me, and said:

"You must excuse me dat I din't be heah to brush your clothes dis mornin', sar; dey had me in de guard-house, last night."

"Had you in the guard-house—what for?"

"Because I was out widout a pass. You see I don' sleep heah, sar, and I was jes gwine down to de boat, 'bout two o'clock, and dey took me, and put me in de guard-house."

"And what kind of accommodations do they give you at the guard-house?"

"Why, dey makes me pay a dollar for 'em. I offered dem two dollars las' night, if dey let me go. I tort dat's de way dey do; make you pay two dollar, or else dey gives you a right smart whippin'; but dey didn'—I don' know why. I tell you, sar, I nebber felt so mortify in all my life, as wen dey lets me out de guard-house dis mornin', right before all de people in dat ar market-place."

"Well, I suppose it was your own fault."

"*No, sar!* not my own fault 'tall, sar; dey ought to gib me a pass; why not? dey knows I's a married man. Do dey tink I's gwine to sleep heah wid dese nasty niggers? No, sar! I lie out dah on de floor in de passage, and catch my deff of cold first. I aint been use to sich treatem. *I's got a master.* My master's member Congress. Wen dat broks up, he mus fine me nodder place mighty quick. I don' stay heah. I's always been a family servant. You see, sar, I aint use to such treatem. Nebber was sole yet in all my life. My missis' fader was worf four hundred tousand dollar, and we had two plantation. Nebber was in a field in my life—allers was in de house ebber since I was a little chile. I was a kine of pet boy, you see, master. I allers wait on my masser myself till my little brudder got big enough; den I want to go 'way. Oh, I'se a wild chile, you see, sar, and I want to clear out and hab some fun to myself. I's a kine of favorite allers to my mistress. She 'ould do anything for me. She wanted to learn me to read, but I'ru too wild. She would gib me a first-rate education, I 'spose, only I's so wild I wouldn'."

"Can't you read at all!"

"Well, I ken read some, but not very well. Dat is, you see, master, dere's *some* of de letters I can't read, not all on 'em I can't; no sar; but I ken read some."

THE CITIZENS.

There were about one hundred passengers on the Fashion, besides a number of poor people and negroes on the lower deck. They were, generally, cotton-planters, going to Mobile on business, or emigrants bound to Texas or Arkansas. They were usually well dressed, but were a rough, coarse style of people, drinking a great deal, and most of the time under a little alcoholic excitement. Not sociable, except when the topics of cotton, land, and negroes, were started; interested, however, in talk about theatres and the turf; very profane; often showing the handles of concealed weapons about their persons, but not quarrelsome, avoiding disputes and altercations, and respectful to one another in forms of words; very ill-informed, except on plantation business; their language very ungrammatical, idiomatic, and extravagant. Their grand characteristics—simplicity of motive, vague, shallow, and purely objective habits of thought; spontaneity and truthfulness of utterance, and bold, self-reliant movement.

With all their individual independence, I soon could perceive a very great homogeneousness of character, by which they were distinguishable from any other people with whom I had before been thrown in contact; and I began to study it with interest, as the Anglo-Saxon development of the Southwest.

I found that, more than any people I had ever seen, they were unrateable by dress, taste, forms, and expenditures. I was perplexed by finding, apparently united in the same individual, the self-possession and confidence of the well equipped gentleman, and the coarseness and low tastes of the uncivilized boor—frankness and reserve, recklessness and self restraint, extravagance, and penuriousness.

There was one man, who "lived, when he was to home," as he told me, "in the Red River Country," in the northeastern part of Texas, having emigrated thither from Alabama, some years before. He was a tall, thin, awkward person, and wore a suit of clothes (probably bought "ready-made") which would have better suited a short, fat figure. Under his waistcoat he carried a large knife, with the hilt generally protruding at the breast. He had been with his family to his former home, to do a little business, and visit his relatives, and was now returning to his plantation. His wife was a pale and harassed looking woman; and he scarce ever paid her the smallest attention, not even sitting near her at the public table. Of his children, however, he seemed very fond; and they had a negro servant in attendance upon them, whom he was constantly scolding and threatening. Having been from home for six weeks, his impatience to return was very great, and was constantly aggravated by the frequent and long continued stoppages of the boat. "Time's money, time's money!" he would be constantly saying, while we were taking on cotton, "time's worth more 'n money to me now; a hundred per cent more, 'cause I left my niggers all alone, not a dam white man within four mile on 'em."

I asked how many negroes he had.

"I've got twenty on 'em to home, and thar they ar! and thar they ar! and thar aint a dam soul of a white fellow within four mile on"em."

"They are picking cotton, I suppose?"

"No, I got through pickin' fore I left."

"What work have they to do, then, now?"

"I set em to clairin', but they aint doin' a dam thing—not a dam thing, they aint; that's wat they are doin', that is—not a dam thing. I know that, as well as you do. That's the reason time's an object. I told the capting so wen I came a board: ' says I, capting, says I, time is in the objective case with me.' No, sir, they aint doin' a dam solitary thing; that's what they are up to. I know that as well as anybody; I do. But I'll make it up, I'll make it up, when I get thar, now you'd better believe."

Once, when a lot of cotton, baled with unusual neatness, was coming on board, and some doubt had been expressed as to the economy of the method of baling, he said very loudly:

"Well, now, I'd be willin' to bet my salvation, that them thar's the heaviest bales that's come on to this boat."

"I'll bet you a hundred dollars of it," answered one.

"Well, if I was in the habit of bettin', I'd do it. I aint a bettin' man. But I am a cotton man, I am, and I don't car who knows it. I know cotton, I do. I'm dam if I know anythin' but cotton. I ought to know cotton, I had. I've been at it ever sin' I was a chile."

"Stranger," he asked me once, "did you ever come up on the Leweezay? She's a right smart, pretty boat, she is, the Leweezay; the best I ever see on the Alabamy river. They wanted me to wait and come down on her, but I told 'em time was in the objective case to me. She is a right pretty boat, and her capting's a high-tone gentleman; haint no objections to find with him—he's a high-tone gentleman, that's what he is. But the pilot—well, damn him! He run her right out of the river, up into the woods—didn't run her in the river, at all. When I go aboard a steam-boat, I like to keep in the river, somewar; but that pilot, he took her right up into the woods.

It was just clairin' land. Clairin' land, and playin' hell ginerally, all night; not follering the river at all. I believe he was drunk. He must have been drunk, for I could keep a boat in the river myself. I'll never go in a boat where the pilot's drunk all the time. I take a glass too much myself, sometimes; but I don't hold two hundred lives in the holler of my hand. I was in my berth, and he run her straight out of the river, slap up into the furest. It threw me clean out of my berth, out onter the floor; I didn't sleep any more while I was aboard. The Leweezay's a right smart, pretty little boat, and her capting's a high-tone gentleman. They hev good livin' aboard of her, too. Haan't no objections on that score; weddin' fixins all the time; but I won't go in a boat war the pilot's drunk. I set some vally on the life of two hundred souls. They wanted to hev me come down on her, but I told 'em time was in the objective case."

There were three young negroes, carried by another Texan, on the deck, outside the cabin. I don't know why they were not allowed to be with the other emigrant slaves, on the lower deck, unless the owner was afraid of their trying to get away, and had no handcuffs small enough for them. They were boys; the oldest twelve or fourteen years old, the youngest not more than seven. They had evidently been bought lately by their present owner, and probably had just been taken from their parents. They lay on the deck and slept, with no bed but the passengers' luggage, and no cover but a single blanket for each. Early one morning, after a very stormy night, when they must have suffered much from the driving rain and cold, I saw their owner with a glass of spirits, giving each a few swallows from it. The older ones smacked their lips, and said, "Tank 'on, massa;" but the little one couldn't drink it, and cried aloud, when he was forced to. The older ones were very playful and quarrelsome, and continually teasing the younger, who seemed very sad, or homesick and sulky. He would get very angry at their mischievous fun, and sometimes strike them. He would then be driven into a corner, where he would lie on his back, and kick at them in a perfect frenzy of anger and grief. The two boys would continue to laugh at him, and frequently the passengers would stand about, and be amused by it. Once, when they had plagued him in this way for some time, he jumped up on to the cotton-bales, and made as if he would have plunged

Engraving of "Slaves Shipping Cotton by Torch Light—River Alabama."

overboard. One of the older boys caught him by the ankle, and held him till his master came and hauled him in, and gave him a severe flogging with a rope's end. A number of passengers collected about them, and I heard several say, "That's what he wants." Red River said to me, "I've been a watchin' that ar boy, and I see what's the matter with him; he's got the devil in him right bad and he'll hev to take a right many of them warmins before it'll be got out."

The crew of the boat, as I have intimated, was composed partly of Irishmen, and partly of negroes; the latter were slaves, and were hired of their owners at $40 a month—the same wages paid to the Irishmen. A dollar of their wages was given to the negroes themselves, for each Sunday they were on the passage. So far as convenient, they were kept at work separately from the white hands; they were also messed separately. On Sunday I observed them dining in a group, on the cotton-bales. The food, which was given to them in tubs, from the kitchen, was various and abundant, consisting of bean-porridge, bacon, corn bread, ship's biscuit, potatoes, duff (pudding), and gravy. There was one knife used only, among ten of them; the bacon was cut and torn into shares; splinters of the bone and of fire-wood were used for forks; the porridge was passed from one to another, and drank out of the tub; but though excessively dirty and beast-like in their appearance and manners, they were good-natured and jocose as usual.

"Heah! you Bill," said one to another, who was on a higher tier of cotton, "pass down do dessart. You! up dar on de hill; de dessart! Augh! don't you know what de dessart be? De duff, you fool."

"Does any of de gemmen want some o' dese potatum?" asked another; and no answer being given, he turned the tub full of potatoes overboard, without any hesitation. It was evident he had never had to think on one day how he should be able to live the next.

Whenever we landed at night or on Sunday, for wood or cotton, there would be many negroes come on board from the neighboring plantations, to sell eggs to the steward.

Sunday was observed by the discontinuance of public gambling in the cabin, and in no other way. At midnight gambling was resumed, and during the whole passage was never at any other time discontinued, night or day, so far as I saw. There were three men that seemed to be professional sharpers, and who probably played into each other's hands. One young man lost all the money he had with him—several hundred dollars.

MOBILE.

. . . .

CHAPTER X

ECONOMICAL EXPERIENCE.

The territorial Government of Alabama was established in 1816 [1817], and in 1818 [1819] she was admitted as a State into the Union. In 1820, her population was 128,000; in 1850, it had increased to 772,000; the increase of the previous ten years having been 30 per cent. (that of South Carolina was 5 per cent.; of Georgia, 31; Mississippi, 60; Michigan, 87;

Wisconsin, 890). A large part of Alabama has yet a strikingly frontier character. Even from the State-house, in the fine and promising town of Montgomery, the eye falls in every direction upon a dense forest, boundless as the sea, and producing in the mind the same solemn sensation. Towns frequently referred to as important points in the stages of your journey, when you reach them, you are surprised to find consist of not more than three or four cabins, a tavern or grocery, a blacksmith's shop, and a stable.

A stranger once meeting a coach, in which I was riding, asked the driver whether it would be prudent for him to pass through one of these places, that we had just come from; he had heard that there were more than fifty cases of small-pox in the town. "There ain't fifty people in the town, nor within ten mile on't," answered the driver, who was a northerner. The best of the country roads are but little better than open passages for strong vehicles through the woods, made by cutting away the trees.

The greater number of planters own from ten to twenty slaves only, though plantations on which from fifty to a hundred are employed are not uncommon, especially on the rich alluvial soils of the southern part of the State. Many of the largest and most productive plantations are extremely unhealthy in summer, and their owners seldom reside upon them, except temporarily. Several of the larger towns, like Montgomery, remarkable in the midst of the wilderness which surrounds them, for the neatness and tasteful character of the houses and gardens which they contain, are in a considerable degree, made up of the residences of gentlemen who own large plantations in the hotter and less healthful parts of the State. Many of these have been educated in the older States, and with minds enlarged and liberalized by travel, they form, with their families, cultivated and attractive society.

Much the larger proportion of the planters of the State live in log-houses, some of them very neat and comfortable, but frequently rude in construction, not *chinked*, with windows unglazed, and wanting in many of the commonest conveniences possessed by the poorest class of Northern farmers and laborers of the older States. Many of those who live in this way, possess considerable numbers of slaves, and are every year buying more. Their early frontier life seems to have destroyed all

"A Southern Planter's Home in Alabama."

capacity to enjoy many of the usual luxuries of civilized life.

Notwithstanding the youth of the State, there is a constant and extensive emigration from it, as well as immigration to it. Large planters, as their stock increases, are always anxious to enlarge the area of their land, and will often pay a high price for that of any poor neighbor, who, embarrassed by debt, can be tempted to move on. There is a rapid tendency in Alabama, as in the older Slave States, to the enlargement of plantations. The poorer class are steadily driven to occupy poor land, or move forward on to the frontier.

In an Address before the Chunnennggee Horticultural Society, by Hon. C. C. Clay, Jr., reported by the author in De Bow's Review, December, 1855, I find the following passage. I need add not a word to it to show how the political experiment of old Virginia, the Carolinas, and Georgia, is being repeated to the same cursed result in young Alabama. The author, it is fair to say, is devoted to the sustentation of Slavery, and would not, for the world, be suspected of favoring any scheme for arresting this havoc of wealth, further than by chemical science:

"I can show you, with sorrow, in the older portions of Alabama, and in my native county of Madison, the sad memorials of the artless and exhausting culture of cotton. Our small planters, after taking the cream off their lands, unable to restore them by rest, manures, or otherwise, are going further west and south, in search of other virgin lands, which they may and will despoil and impoverish in like manner. Our wealthier planters, with greater means and no more skill, are buying out their poorer neighbors, extending their plantations, and adding to their slave force. The wealthy few, who are able to live on smaller profits, and to give their blasted fields some rest, are thus pushing off the many, who are merely independent.

"Of the twenty millions of dollars annually realized from the sales of the cotton crop of Alabama, nearly all not expended in supporting the producers is reinvested in land and negroes. Thus the white population has decreased, and the slave increased, almost *pari passu* in several counties of our State. In 1825, Madison county cast about 3,000 votes; now she cannot cast exceeding 2,300. In traversing that county one will discover numerous farm-houses, once the abode of industrious and intelligent freemen, now occupied by slaves, or tenantless, deserted, and dilapidated; he will observe fields, once fertile, now unfenced, abandoned, and covered with those evil harbingers—fox-tail and broom-sedge; he will see the moss growing on the mouldering walls of once thrifty villages; and will find 'one only master grasps the whole domain' that once furnished happy homes for a dozen white families. Indeed, a country in its infancy, where, fifty years ago, scarce a forest tree had been felled by the axe of the pioneer, is already exhibiting the painful signs of senility and decay, apparent in Virginia and the Carolinas; the freshness of its agricultural glory in gone; the vigor of its youth is extinct, and the spirit of desolation seems brooding over it."

18

Robert Everest

January 1854

Robert Everest, a graduate of Oxford, served in Bengal as a chaplain of the East India Company. He was opposed to slavery, but he did believe that Southern plantation slaves were no worse off than English rural workers. This was no mere offhand opinion. After all, Everest's scholarly work included *On the Influence of Social Degradation in Producing Pauperism and Crime, as Exemplified in the Free Colored Citizens and Foreigners in the United States.* This treatise, inspired by his similar work in British India, and read to London's Statistical Society in 1854 and printed in the *Journal of the Statistical Society of London* in 1855, was also printed in the Southern *De Bose Review* during the same year.

Although the Reverend Everest had a marked scholarly inclination, he was also interested in local color and atmosphere—the state of the roads, life on riverboats, card playing, dancing, and dueling. The short passage below illustrates both interests.

Robert Everest, *A Journey Through the United States and Part of Canada* (London: John Chapman, 1855), 113–115.

CHAPTER X

After a very short stay [in Mobile], I left by the steamer on the Alabama river for Montgomery. This river is not above 80 yards to 100 yards wide, and, where it issues from the swamp, is enclosed between high banks covered with forest, and runs at a rapid rate. Its breadth does not vary all the way to Montgomery, but its steep banks show at times sections of red and variegated marl, similar to what I had seen between Philadelphia and

Painting of the second Capitol designed by Barachias Holt of Maine. This painting of the 1851 building dates from the 1850s.

Washington. Montgomery, at which we arrived after a voyage of forty hours, is pleasantly situated upon a hill of these marly strata, 50 feet or more above the level of the river. The streets are well laid out, at right angles to each other, as in most American towns, but as the roadway is neither paved nor macadamized, and the weather happened to be wet when I was there, it was a perfect quagmire, through which beasts of every kind struggled as they could.

The Capitol is well situated on an eminence, and, as the Legislature was sitting, I went to have a look at them.

I entered a large circular chamber, below a dome, where a number of members were sitting at desks with pens, ink, and paper before them. These desks are arranged in circular lines, as seats in a theatre are, the "Chair" occupying the spot that in the theatre would be the centre front of the stage. This form appears to be general in the American Houses of Legislature, and naturally so, for it is well known that this is the form of building when enables the greatest numbers of persons to hear, and to be heard with ease. Strange to say, the example has not been followed in England, though, at the time of rebuilding the Houses of Parliament, an opportunity was afforded of making a change in the shape of the chambers.

From the Capitol the view extends over a thick forest as far as the eye can reach. The State of Alabama is but thinly inhabited, the number of inhabitants to a square mile not being above fifteen, by the last Census of 1850.

The beds of red and variegated marl here are said to belong to the eocene formation.

When the time came for my departure, I was dragged through the quagmire about a mile in a coach to the railway station, set down with no shelter from the sky on a rainy day, and placed in a train that managed to accomplish 88 miles in about eight hours. Down poured the rain during these eight hours, and, except occasional clearings of cotton fields, all that could be seen was pine forest and swamp, and the blue mist that had settled down upon them. On arriving at our journey's end, West Point, we were again set down in the rain, and had to make the best of our way through the mud to a wooden shed near, denominated the Hotel, where we slept. The afternoon was so warm, that windows were thrown open, and people were sitting outside the house, smoking (17th January).

19

James Redpath

November–December 1854

JAMES REDPATH (1833–1889) was Scottish-born, but emigrated to the United States in his teens. He worked for Horace Greeley as a reporter for the *New York Tribune*. In 1855, Redpath moved to Kansas and worked with John Brown to ensure that Kansas would enter the Union as a free state. Subsequently, he not only participated in a daring, but futile attempt to rescue Brown at Harpers Ferry, but he also wrote Brown's first biography, as well as dedicated *Roving Editor* to Captain John Brown. After visiting Haiti in 1860, he successfully lobbied the United States government to recognize the black republic. However, he abandoned his effort to get skilled, free blacks to immigrate to Haiti. During the Civil War, Redpath served as a war correspondent, and then, in 1865, as the first public schools superintendent in Charleston, South Carolina. He quickly lost this job, because he urged the Johnson administration to protect freedmen's rights.

Redpath's varied career took even more unusual turns when he organized one of the country's first professional lecture booking agencies. Redpath himself lectured in Ireland in the 1880s, returning to the United States as an Irish nationalist. His most unusual turn, however, was his late nineteenth-century friendship with Jefferson Davis. That relationship began when Redpath convinced Davis to write for the *North American Review*, which Redpath edited. In time, he spent several months in Davis's house near Biloxi, helped Davis with his history of the Confederacy, and even helped Davis's widow with her husband's biography.

In the 1850s, Redpath visited the South three times. The intent of the extreme abolitionist was to test his views on Southern slavery. His research method was unique: he walked, including a trip from Richmond to Montgomery. Walking afforded opportunities to interview thousands of slaves. He travelled incognito, and published his letters first in *New York National Anti-Slavery Standard* under the pseudonym John Ball Jr., referring to the English priest John Ball, one of the three leaders of the Peasants' Revolt of 1381. In fact, Redpath himself advocated simultaneous slave revolts in the South. He exhibited the moral certainty of a fanatic, believing that evil deserved evil.

James Redpath, *Roving Editor: or, Talks with Slaves in the Southern States* (New York: A. B. Burdick, 1859), 171–176.

ALABAMA.

I walked the entire distance from Atlanta, Georgia, to Montgomery, Alabama. As I intend to revisit that country at the earliest opportunity, I will not here narrate my adventures on this journey. They would probably discover me—not my mere name, but personality. That I desire to avoid. Alabama, as the reader most probably is aware, is preeminently the Assassin State; for it has still on the pages of its statute book a law authorizing the payment of $5,000 for the head of Mr. Garrison, dead or alive.

The result of my journey are thus recorded in a letter from Montgomery:

CONTENTMENT OF SLAVES IN ALABAMA.

I have spoken with hundreds of slaves in Alabama, but never yet met *one* contented with his position under the "peculiar" constitutions of the South. But neither have I met with many slaves who are actively discontented with involuntary servitude. Their discontent is passive only. They neither hope, nor grumble, nor threaten. I never advised a single slave either in Georgia or Alabama to run away. It is too great a responsibility to incur. The distance is too far; the opportunities and chances of escape too few. The slaves, I found, regard themselves as the victims of a system of injustice from which the only earthly hope of escape is—*the grave!*

RAILROAD HANDS.

The shareholders of the railroad from West Point, Georgia, to Montgomery, Alabama, own all the slaves who are employed in grading, pumping, wood cutting, engine firing, and in other necessary labors along the line. These men are the most favored sons of Africa *employed in the country*, in the States of Alabama or Georgia. They are hard worked from sun to sun, and from Christmas to Christmas, but they are well fed and clothed, and comfortably lodged—comfortably, that is for negro slaves.

THEIR ALLOWANCE.

They receive five pounds of pork, a pint of molasses, and one peck of meal each per week; three suits of clothes, a blanket and a hat a year. But they have no wives. They are chiefly by birth Virginians, and were nearly all bought in the Old Dominion eleven years ago. The majority that I spoke with were married men and fathers at the time of the purchase; but, as the railroad company had no need of female servants, *their* "Domestic Institutions" were broken up, and—wifeless and childless—the poor "fellows" (as they are called), were transported south, and condemned for life to Alabama celibacy and adultery. Of course, He who, amid the lightnings of Mount Sinai, uttered the command, "Thou shalt not commit adultery," was the founder of the system of slavery in America which breeds such crimes, and many others of the same character, but far more odious in their nature! Of course? Don't the Southern clergy and the Rev. South-Side Adams, of Instantaneous Conversion and Instantaneous Rendition notoriety, announce the fact? And don't they know?

MARRIAGE AND SLAVERY.

Several of these hands, as they frankly owned, have cohabited with plantation slaves since their arrival in Alabama. All of them, of course, resemble Napoleon in one respect—they are "no Capuchins." One of them—a bachelor when sold, and who had been clerically married here—remarked to me:

"Yes, mass'r, I'se been married; but it's no satisfaction for a man in this country."

"Why?"

"'Cause, mass'r," he replied, "you see white folks here don't know nothin' 'bout farmin'. Dey buy a place and use it up in two or tree years, and den dey go away agin. So we's never sartin of our girls 'bove a year or two."

THE RICH SLAVE.

When about fifty miles distant from Montgomery, I saw a young man of color, well dressed—rather a dandy, in fact—walking along the road in company with a country-looking slave, near the railroad depot. I overtook him and soon began to inquire into his history. He spoke our language as correctly as any educated man does in ordinary conversation. He was a manly looking person and very intelligent.

He was a slave; by trade a carpenter. He hired his own time—that is to say, he paid his owner $300 annually as body rent, boarded and clothed himself, and retained whatever money he made after defraying expenses. He was twenty-eight years of age. Last year he saved $100. Altogether, since he first cherished a hope of purchasing his freedom, he had succeeded in saving $930.

"How much does your boss ask for you?"

"He said he would not sell me for less than $2,500. He was offered $2,000 cash down. I hope to buy myself for less. I was raised with him from a child, and I expect that he will let me buy my freedom for $2,400 on that account."

"$2,400!" I exclaimed, "and you have only got $900 yet. Why it will take you fourteen years to buy yourself at that rate."

"I know that, sir," he replied, "but I can't help myself; *you see he has the advantage of me.*"

"Yes," I returned, "but you have got $930 the advantage of him. Once on the road, you could travel rapidly to the North, as you could easily pay all your expenses, and would not have to run the ordinary risks of a runaway. If I was in your place," I added, "I would see your boss in a hotter climate than this, before I would pay him the first red cent. Can't you get any one to write you your free papers?"

"That's what I want, sir," he said—his eyes flashed as he looked on me and said it—"but I'm afraid to ask: I dare not trust any of the white men I know."

"I'll write them," I replied, "if you will get me free papers to copy from. I don't know how free papers are worded; but if you will show them to me, I will willingly make out yours."

He joyfully promised to furnish me with the "copy" desired, and appointed a place of meeting in Montgomery.

Alas for the poor fellow! Either I mistook the place of rendezvous, or, fearing betrayal, he was afraid to meet me.

OTHER SLAVES AND SLAVE SALES.

My washerwoman in Montgomery hired her own time also. She paid her owner $200 a year; lived in a house rented by herself; was entirely self-supported in every respect.

Another man I spoke with—a plasterer—paid his owner $600 annually. He was a very intelligent and skillful mechanic. He would have sold for $4,000.

These persons never see their owners, excepting only when they pay their body-rent. Of course, this demonstrates that the negroes need a master to take care of them. And does it not prove, too, that American slavery is a *patriarchal* institution, with a vengeance and a half?

The first things that I saw on entering Montgomery were three large posters, whose captions read respectively thus:

"Negroes at auction!"

"Negroes at auction!"

"Negroes for sale!"

Three distinct sales of immortal souls within a few days were thus unblushingly announced. I saw two of them. In one instance, the auctioneer turned, as coolly as an iceberg incarnate, from the last of the negroes whom he sold, to a mule with a buggy and harness. Hardly had the word—"Gone!" escaped his lips, as he finished the sale of the "fellow," than he began:

"*The next lot* that I shall offer you, gentlemen, is a mule with a buggy and harness. This lot," etc.

The negroes brought very high prices. It is interesting to observe how the enlargement of commercial relations makes the interest of one nation the interest of every one with which it has extended intercourse. The Eastern [Crimean] war, which England was waging at the time, was the immediate cause of these inhuman auctions. Cotton was selling at so very reduced a figure, that many of the planters were compelled to dispose of a portion of their human live stock, in order to provide subsistence for the others. And this, you know, is one of the beauties of this beautiful institution.

A GODLY CITY.

Montgomery is a very handsome city. It supports two churches, one weekly (temperance), one tri-weekly, and two daily papers. Population, at that time, nearly nine thousand. It is the capital of Alabama.

Montgomery, albeit, is a very godly city. It is true that its citizens sell human beings on week days; but then—and let it be remembered to its lasting honor—it imposes a fine of thirteen dollars for every separate offence and weed, on any and every unrighteous dealer who *sells a cigar on Sunday!*

Let us smoke!

20

Robert Russell

February 1855

Robert Russell (d. 1871), a British naturalist, read widely in government publications and agricultural journals. The excerpt below reflects his interests in soil conditions, erosion, and exhausted land. The book's title and first sentences of the excerpt also reveal his interest in climate; not surprisingly, he lectured at the Smithsonian Institution on North American climate.

Robert Russell, *North America: Its Agriculture and Climate* (Edinburgh: Adam and Charles Black, 1857), 296–300.

I reached Montgomery, the capital of Alabama, on the night of the 27th February, and started early next morning by the train for the east. The temperature was several degrees below the freezing point, and a thick hoar-frost covered the ground. I got out of the train about six miles to the east of the town; and leaving my portmanteau in the house of one of the plantation overseers, walked about eight miles to the south to visit Dr. Cloud, the editor of the "Cotton Plant." The soil in this district is far from being rich, and the most of the plantations I passed were small. The usual number of working hands was from six to twelve, but in some cases there were even fewer. Small plantations, as has been already pointed out, are invariably found on the secondary descriptions of land.

The soil in the neighbourhood of Montgomery rests upon the cretaceous formation, which is succeeded by the primary, a few miles to the eastward. While the soils over the immense area of the granitic formations in the New England States and the British Possessions are stony and poor, the larger extent of the same class of rocks in the south are covered by soils of moderate fertility. This arises from the fact that the primary rocks in the Southern States having decomposed *in situ*, and not having been subjected to denudation, afford an immense depth of clay and sand. The primary and tertiary soils have a considerable resemblance to each other in lithological character. The surface soil on both formations is often somewhat sandy, from a foot to a foot and a half deep, and contains only a small quantity of vegetable matter. It is remarkable, that the subsoil consists of a siliceous clay, which is thus covered by the sandy soil over an area as large as the whole of England. The geological question arises, How could such an immense stretch of country have become covered with this thin stratum of sand, while the subsoil is so opposite, and, at the same time, homogeneous in its character? I remarked to Dr. Cloud that it had apparently arisen from the washing away of the clay out of the surface soil by the rains, the sand, which the clayey subsoil contained in abundance, being left behind. I have since observed, however, that Sir Charles Lyell discusses some interesting phenomena connected with the geology of Alabama and Georgia; and the peculiar features of the soil and subsoil which I have just described may assist in supporting certain views he puts forth respecting the condition of the surface of the country as it was gradually raised above the ocean.

Sir C. Lyell alludes to the singular phenomenon in the neighbourhood of Milledgeville, in Georgia, of gneiss and mica schist decomposed *in situ* to an immense depth, and also to the surprising extent of some of the modern ravines excavated by the rains since the country has been cleared of timber and cultivated. One of these measured no less than 55 feet in depth, 300 yards in length, and varied in width from 20 to 180 feet; yet, strange to say, twenty years before it had no existence. The walls of this chasm consist of "beds of clay and sand, red, white, yellow, and green, produced by the decomposition *in situ* of hornblendic gneiss, with layers and veins of quartz, as before mentioned, and of a rock consisting of quartz and felspar, which remain entire, to prove that the whole mass was once crystalline."

"I infer, from the rapidity of the denudation caused here by running water after the clearing or removal of wood, that this country has always been covered with a dense forest, from the remote time when it first emerged from the sea. However long may have been the period of upheaval required to raise the massive tertiary strata to the height of more than 600 feet, we may conclude that the surface has been protected by more than a mere covering of herbage, from the effects of the sudden flowing off of the rain water."

"I know it may be contended that, when the granite and gneiss first rose as islands out of the sea, they may have consisted entirely of hard rock which resisted denudation, and therefore we can only affirm that the forest has been continuous from the time of the decomposition and softening of the upper portion of these rocks. But I may reply that similar effects are observable, even on a grander scale, in recently excavated ravines, seventy or eighty feet deep, in some newly cleared parts of the tertiary regions of Alabama, as in Clarke county, for example, and also in some of the cretaceous strata of loose gravel, sand, and clay, in the same state at Tuscaloeza. These are at a much greater height above the sea, and must, from the first, have been as destructible as they are now."

This, it appears to me, is sound reasoning. In fact, as these tertiary beds were gradually raised above the sea, they were quickly covered by land plants, which protected their soft surface from denudation by rains, a process which is now found, in many regions, to take place to a great extent where the land is brought under the plough. Might not the sandy surface soil which covers such an immense area have formed the beach as the waters retired, the clayey particles being then washed out by the tides and waves of the sea?

Pines are the chief trees in the forests where the sandy soil prevails; but when it approaches more to a loam, oak and hickory also make their appearance. In all cases in which the soil has been washed and exhausted, the hard-wood trees, as under the same circumstances in the Natchez uplands, cease to spring up; but pines occupy the ground. This fact furnishes another instance of the influence of the physical condition of soils on the growth of different kinds of trees. Betwixt Montgomery and Atlanta, in Georgia, oak and hickory predominate in many places in the natural forest; but none of the land seemed to be at all equal in natural fertility to the uplands of Natchez.

Dr. Cloud's plantation is about 800 feet above the level of the sea. He was sanguine that the soil in his neighbourhood admitted of great improvement by ploughing deep and bringing up a portion of the clayey subsoil to the surface; and the cotton plant is said to be productive on such land when well manured. But the radical defect of the soils, in this district as well as throughout the cotton region in Georgia and the Carolinas, is their unfitness for growing good grasses. This renders the raising of stock of all kinds expensive; and when the fields are allowed to lie waste for some years to recruit their productive powers, they are, during the time, in a great measure worthless. On some of the waste lands here the grasses were from two to three feet in height; but their hard siliceous stems had been untouched by cattle in summer, and, being now dry and withered, imparted a most thriftless aspect to the country.

Agricultural information is well diffused among cultivators in the United States. All of them, both in the North and South, read agricultural papers, and the matter of one journal is commonly transferred to the others. A great uniformity of management thus prevails, where the soil and climate are similar. Horizontal cultivation is as universal in Alabama as it is in the uplands of Natchez, where it was first adopted. The compact subsoils here cause washing, and the rapid deterioration of the natural capabilities of the land ensues, unless it is naturally level or laid carefully off in level ridges. I was well pleased at the skilful manner in which a negro, with one mule in his plough, was drawing horizontal ridges, of about four feet in width, on a slightly undulating field. Little wheat is yet raised at this elevation above the sea; one small field, of about an acre, was on the plantation; the frosts at night were keeping it in check; but it was about six inches in length, and would be ready for harvest by the end of May, and a crop of Indian corn might be afterwards got.

Having spent an agreeable and instructive day with Dr. Cloud, I left early next morning for the railway, and making a signal for the train to stop, got into the cars for Washington, a distance of upwards of 900 miles. This journey occupied three days and three nights. The appearance of the country was most monotonous.

21

Amelia Murray

May 1855

Amelia Matilda Murray (1795–1884) was well-known in British society, not only because she had served as a lady-in-waiting to Queen Victoria, but also because she was an artist, writer, and botanist. Initially, she did not intend to write a book on her travels, yet she wrote one of the best British travel books of the time. The Honorable Amelia Murray's interests and published comments are catholic: architecture, social life, church services, as well as the usual interest in transportation and hotels, and flora, fauna and fossils. Before her travels to Cuba and the American South, her view of slavery was more definite than the conventional antislavery view of Europeans of the time, she was an abolitionist. She shocked both herself and her friends by altering her perception of slavery: judging that Southern house slaves were better clothed and fed than British apprentices and that Southern slaves were less discontented than Northern free blacks. Furthermore, she concluded that blacks were morally and intellectually inferior to whites and must, therefore, be governed. Considering this conclusion, Murray believed that the condition of Southern slaves was as best as could be expected from a practical standpoint.

Amelia M. Murray, *Letters from the United States, Cuba and Canada* (New York: G. P. Putnam and Company, 1856), 302–306.

LETTER XXV.

ATLANTA, ALABAMA, U.S.,}
May 7, 1855.}

MY DEAR FRIENDS,—

After five days' hard travelling, we got here this evening—I should say five days and three nights; for with the exception of one night's rest at Mobile, and one (till five this morning) at Montgomery, since leaving New Orleans, on Thursday last, we have never paused an hour anywhere. Night-work is the only serious obstacle to journeying in America: it is very fatiguing, and where there is a pretty country to pass through, very disappointing to strangers; both in Texas and Alabama this evil at present is incorrigible; because, through wide districts, there are no places to pause at, and the mail being the only means of conveyance, of course it cannot be detained for any one. I might have attempted to get up the Alabama River from Mobile, but the water being low, there was considerable risk of grounding for some days upon sandbanks; besides which, I see more of the country and of the vegetation by coach-travelling; and although it is often very tantalizing to pass by trees, and shrubs, and flowers, either new or rare, without being able to get at them, still it is something to observe the botanical features of a district; and by taking every opportunity, during a change of horses or a stop for meals, I have secured several interesting specimens, and sometimes get a sketch.

. . . Next day, Saturday, a steamer received us on board, and leaving Mobile Bay, we went up the river Tensaw, a stream beautiful as the Altamaha, and bordered by woods far exceeding those of Georgia: live oaks, catalpas, magnolias (as large as elms), just come into blow; the macrophylla with its flower still sweeter and more splendid than the grandiflora, melias, gleditzchias, cedars, sweet and black gum-trees, &c., with huge alligators occasionally basking beneath these verdant shores, and elegant birds flying above them.

At Stockport we found two roomy four-horse coaches waiting for passengers: five gentlemen, R——, and I took possession of one intended to hold nine inside, which would have been close packing; so we were fortunate in not being quite as much cramped as we might have been. Nearly the whole two hundred miles to this place is deep sand, varying from white to red; at first, through pine barrens like those of Florida, only covering a rolling country instead of a flat one; but within fifty miles of

Montgomery the forest becomes as various, and as rich, and as hilly, as that of the eastern part of Texas, and much resembling it in character and in soil—a red iron-sand. At one of the little post-houses I got a nodule of iron ore, which they said was plentiful in the neighbourhood. By midnight we arrived at Montgomery, a clean looking, gas-lit town, of which I could not see a great deal, for it was necessary to be in the railroad cars by six the next morning. A short distance from Montgomery the line was bordered on each side by hedges of Cherokee roses, vivid evergreens with single white blossoms, and the foliage so thick that it is said not even a snake can get through it: then we went by the prettiest scenery of all—passing the rivers Coosa and Tallapoosa, and near the spot where General Jackson fought his 'Battle of the Horseshoe' with the Cherokees and Choctaws. One of my poor little horny, crusty reptiles is dead, in spite of all the care I could bestow upon him. I fear the other will not survive the long journey in prospect; perhaps it would be better that these creatures should travel at the usual season of their torpidity; now, the sun makes them too much inclined for an active life, and they evidently think it necessary to eat flies, whereas, in the winter season, that would not be requisite.

. . . During my last passage in the steamer from Mobile, a black woman came and sat down by me in the stern of the vessel. From what we hear in England, I imagined negroes were kept at a distance. That is the case in the Northern States, but in the South they are at your elbow everywhere, and always seek conversation. This was an old nurse, an aunty, or mammy, as they are sometimes called (all ancient women of the darky kind here are addressed as aunties). She was very communicative, told me she had a young mistress in Texas (sisters have sometimes a common property in slaves left by their parents); that she was very fond of this master and mistress, and she ran on as follows—'But there 'tis hard to be divided from t'other; but then people must have their 'flictions in this world. When I was a young girl, there, I used sometimes to fancy 'twould be a fine thing to be free; but, there, I don't now think 'twould be mighty fine at all; there, I have everything I want in the wide world, 'cept jewellery, and that I don't want at all now, and, there (some of the coloured people have such a lot of jewellery you can't think); I say, Cissy, now (addressing one of her charges) don't go for to tumble over there; now if you gets into the water, we sha'n't have you a bit more, and then your poor old aunty will die of it—that she will—and won't see her no more. I say, missus, I don't let master keep my children up o'nights as some of their papas and mammas do: I says, 'Master, it sha'n't be, it sha'n't—it isn't fit for they little ones as ought to be in their beds;' and so my children have got colours in their faces, that they does.. I asked her what she thought of slaves being free here: her reply was, 'I say, missus, it does 'em no good, nor any one else. If people has a fancy to make 'em free, send 'em to Africa, the place they comed from, I say. Why, missus, these free niggers are half their time bad niggers; and they does insult they niggers as keeps to their own masters and mistresses, and are mighty better and happier too, and that makes 'em mad to see. It is not right, missus, by the 'spectable slaves to have them there free niggers, with their jewellery, and their flowers, and their 'bacco, and their drink, idling about saucy and idle, it gives the dark people a bad 'kracter; and I say, missus, it isn't right. Send 'em away, I say, and then they may go and sit in the sun and do nothing, just as the half of them do.' So she ran on in a stream of talk, all much to the same purpose. One question to set these people off is generally enough to have the benefit of all their thoughts; but it is better to keep one's own opinions in the background, for they are so imitative, they will often reflect you if they can. The day before yesterday, I heard of an intelligent negro just freed by his master, after thirty-six years' good service. He was fifteen when brought over, remembered his native tongue, and intends to return to Africa. He strongly expresses his gratitude for having been brought over to America, and says, 'Master, don't you let white masters and mistresses hurt the Slavery Institution. I say, Master, it be *Good* Almighty's school for the coloured people it be, that He have made. Why, Massa, what would such a man as me have been without the slave merchant? How should me have got a bit of education as me have? And now go and try to give a bit to the race out there, who would a bring us over? I say, Master, we should ha' been worse than slaves, but for the Slavery Institution that brought us here to know how to work, and to hear about the good Almighty, and to know about what we should never have known in our own country. No, Massa, don't hurt the Slave Institution.' What would Mrs. Stowe say to this Uncle Tom? for he is the nearest to Uncle Tom of any negro I have heard of, and he will make a capital African missionary.

22

John Shaw

January 1856

John Shaw, a native of Boston, Lincolnshire, became a fellow of both the Geological Society and Linnean Society of London. The English physician published five travel books between 1856 and 1861. None was favorably received by the London critics. *Ramble* was called "at once superficial and pretentious," and this was mild compared to other criticism. Not only did Dr. Shaw dislike slavery, the common sentiment, but he also saw the South with condescension, yet with candor and humor.

John Shaw, *A Ramble Through the United States, Canada, and the West Indies* (London: J. F. Hope, 1856), 210–215.

Arrived at Montgomery, in the state of Alabama, a town situate in the middle of a beautiful bog, where, in the summer time, bilious, intermittent, and yellow fevers invariably prevail. It was during the winter season, in the month of January, that the thermometer stood at 70° at Montgomery, and a thunder-storm— such an one as I had never previously seen—having more similarity to a great universal waterfall, accompanied with constant flashes of lightning (not dissimilar to spirit of wine, ignited), is almost without intermission illuminating the town in such a manner that one could only compare it to the rising and setting of the sun in rapid succession. I attended a concert at the Montgomery Hotel, given by four American vocalists. Among the songs sang upon the occasion, was one giving an account of John Bull taxing the tea, with other allusions to the revolutionary times, which called forth not so much applause as I anticipated. Another of them was to the effect of "Put the kettle on;" "Loud blow the bellows;" "If John Bull [the English equivalent of the American Uncle Sam] should come upon our coast, we will give him gunpowder tea"—this latter also failed in eliciting any amount of marked approbation; fully showing that the people of the town were well disposed towards John Bull; and that there, at all events, the war-movement was not popular. The singers, before commencing their performance, made no salutation, and also finished their songs without bowing.

January 10th. Embarked on board the Marengo steam-boat, at Montgomery, in the State of Alabama, and sailed down a river named after the State, a distance of 500 miles, for the sum of *£1*, with provisions included. This was cheap enough. Travelling in the United States where the passengers do not exist in great numbers, I think may be considered dear. The steam-boat was one with a high-pressure engine, one of the finest I ever saw; and I must confess that the thundering rush of steam, vomited through her capacious pipes, rather startled me the first time I heard it, especially when I pictured to my imagination the possibility of an explosion, an event too frequently resulting from the bad management of these high-pressure steamers. The peculiarity of her construction was not a little interesting; for the accommodations were all above deck, instead of below. The great saloon, which extended from one end of the boat to the other, was very handsomely fitted up, and could not fail in calling forth the admiration of the traveller, especially to a foreigner viewing it for the first time. The berths were differently placed to the Hudson steamers, in having the beds fixed in a small room, with its door and number upon it. The group of passengers was, as might be expected, very various, and even variegated, for some of them wore white blanket coats, embroidered at the edges with blue and scarlet, some in entirely blue coats, and others in red ones. These gentlemen, so remarkable for their variegated costumes, were from the far west. I conversed with many of them without meeting an intentionally rude or disagreeable individual. I was informed that in this mixed group there were gamblers, blacklegs, and other idlers, who are called, in the States, Loafers. I met with the greatest possible politeness and attention from the passengers, especially when I informed them that I was a Britisher, as they designate an Englishman; and I am bound to assert, to do them justice, that, although the Southern gentleman lives in a poorer and less cultivated country than his brethren of the North, and in whose States education has not advanced so much as in the New England States, and where the slave is bought and sold like a pig or a house, yet he is a much more communicative and more agreeable travelling companion than the men of the Northern States. I here experienced, for the first time, an offer to pass or leave a dish at the table—a thing very unusual in the Northern States; or, if it is the custom, I had the misfortune not to have an opportunity of observing it. I came in contact but with one of the ladies, and I am bound to confess that I never, upon any occasion, in any country, fell in with a more agreeable, intelligent, and amiable woman; so much so, that I deeply regretted parting with her.

I observed, sitting opposite to me at meals, a youth with a fine expression of countenance, dressed very shabbily in his white blanket coat, fringed with blue, with long hair flowing wildly over his shoulders, whose appearance, most favorably conjectured, could not have passed for any individual higher in the scale than a working man: afterwards, however, I found this individual bowing away in pretty good style on the violin, and, not content with that display of his musical abilities, further commenced and ended a good piece upon the piano, to the great astonishment as well as delight of the beholders and listeners; proving the difficulty of accurately judging a man from his dress and appearance.

The Alabama, down which I sailed to Mobile, like most of the American rivers, is very tortuous in its course, but differed in another respect, viz. that of unusual narrowness, as well as being bounded by the most monotonous, swampy low ground, filled with trees, from whose branches dangled a long thready mass of vegetable matter (a species of lichen), in some instances more than a foot in length; and so completely and invariably were they furnished with it, that there was scarcely to be found a tree without these waving and floating and most peculiar appendages. This appearance is peculiar to the trees of the Southern States. We passed 500 miles of this most monotonous scene, in a river which, if appropriately named, ought to have been called the liquid-mud river, without observing a decent house on its banks, or a change of scene to relieve the eye, without an inch of cultivated land, nothing but swamp and wood, surrounded and soaked in stagnant water, which contained all the obnoxious sources of those endemic disorders which too powerfully attack both the native and the foreigner. In this river, during the summer season, might be seen the alligator, lazily lolling on logs of wood, as if he were an animal of such delicate constitution as only to be capable of enduring the fresh breezes of summer, at the most enlivening period of the year. This river and the alligator are well matched; for I think it would be with difficulty that one could encounter two uglier things in the domains of universal nature.

I arrived at Mobile early in the morning. I found this climate the most delightful imaginable, although in the summer season it would be certain death for a foreigner to inhale its poisonous atmosphere. I never felt in England during the summer season such an agreeable temperature and climate as I experienced at Mobile at their coldest season of the year. The town is situated not far from the Gulph of Mexico, and is remarkable for possessing a shifting population, like that of a watering place. The Northerners are the great visitors during the winter months, who carry on an extensive speculation in cotton, and who quit the town as soon as the unhealthy season commences.

23

Carlton Holmes Rogers

April 1856

Carlton Holmes Rogers (circa 1818–1884) of New York State wrote one of the period's better travel books. He includes the expected observations on travel conditions, public institutions, etc., but unusual for the time, he was not as interested in slavery as were most travel writers. The following passage, however, does contrast slavery in Cuba and the American South. Even more unusual was his sympathetic treatment of poor whites. He made the effort to paint both the worst and the best, the latter deviating from convention.

Carlton Holmes Rogers, *Incidents of Travel in the Southern States and Cuba* (New York: R. Craighead, Publishers, 1862), 241–256.

After leaving Columbus we crossed the Chattahoochee River into Alabama, and proceeded by rail to this city, which is the capital of this state, and next in commercial importance to Mobile. When we entered Alabama, the appearance of the country began to improve. The soil was better; the agricultural districts richer; the scenery more varied; and all kinds of vegetation further advanced. Swelling hills crowned with trees in full foliage, and rich valleys and fertile plains clad in living verdure, with tiny streams meandering in the distance, formed a picture on which the eye delighted to linger.

I arrived in this city late in the afternoon, and secured a room at one of the best hotels, although it does not compare favorably with our third-rate New York hotels, and is not such as a stranger would expect to find in a town as large as this, and of equal commercial and political importance. I shall remain here for several days, and will write again before I take my departure. * * *

LETTER XVI.

MONTGOMERY, *April,* 1856.

There is a dreamy languor in the climate of the South, which indisposes one to exertion, and even the effort of letter writing—which, under ordinary circumstances, is but "a labor of love"—appears to me, at this time, to be an almost herculean task.

Montgomery is located at the head of steamboat navigation on the Alabama River, three hundred and thirty-one miles from Mobile, and has a population of about ten thousand. It is the western terminus of the Montgomery and West Point railroad, and has water communication with several important places. Its commerce is based mainly upon corn and cotton, about one hundred thousand bales of the fleecy product being annually shipped at this place. In the way of manufactures, Montgomery does but little, except, as some one has said, "to manufacture the politics of the State." It is the great political centre of the Gulf States, and the congregating place for southern politicians, newspaper reporters, office-seekers, *et hoc genus omne.*

The city is beautifully situated. The business portion is in a valley extending nearly to the river; while the capitol occupies an eminence overlooking the lower part of the city, and the country which lies beyond it. Encircling this valley is a succession of hills and gentle undulations, forming as it were a natural amphitheatre dotted with villas and country-seats. I made the circuit on horseback. Every eminence that I ascended, revealed some new object to admire; some Italian villa or cottage *orné* peeping out from its wilderness of shrubbery, or a lordly mansion reposing in dignity beneath the perennial shade of giant live-oaks—the acknowledged monarchs of the southern forests. I rode for several hours through these delightfully picturesque suburbs, and had my admiration excited at every step. Nature created this a paradise. Art adorned and beautified it. But in this flowery Eden the trail of the serpent is visible. Notwithstanding its elevated location, the city is said to be quite unhealthy. The yellow fever, that pestilential scourge of the South, prevails here at times to an alarming extent, and other diseases less virulent in their nature seem to be, as it were, indigenous to this locality.

During my rambles I came to a spot of such quiet beauty and loveliness, that I stopped and gazed upon it for a long time in silent admiration. It was an inclosure of two or three acres, on whose swelling bosom of velvet softness reposed a modest little cottage almost buried in a wilderness of foliage and flowers. Standing near were two parental oaks, the protecting deities of the place, whose gigantic, out-stretched limbs, gnarled and defiant, strove in vain to meet above, and hide their offspring from the face of the over-arching sky. Encircling this classic retreat was a perennial hedge almost smothered in the embrace of creeping vines and plants in full bloom. Roses of various hues, and the fragrant honeysuckle and yellow flowering jasmine, were intermingled, yielding alike their perfume to the breeze, and filling the surrounding air with the purest life.

"A sweeter spot on earth was never found:
I looked and looked, and still with new delight,
Such joy my soul, such pleasures filled my sight."

Time flew on angels' wings, and the shades of evening were fast gathering, before I became conscious of the lateness of the hour. Returning to the hotel, I supped, and then wandered in the streets, which were as brilliant as handsome ladies and gas could make them. The shops and stores are all of modern style, and apparently well stocked with fashionable goods. Progress is unmistakably written on everything. Fogyism, that ancient enemy of enterprise and improvement, had fled at the first scream of the steam-whistle, and has not been seen here since. It is evidently a fast city, with its fast horses, fast men, and fast women. The latter are said to be the best in a long race, and generally manage to distance all their competitors. I find that two-forty is the standard time here among bipeds as well as quadrupeds, and those of less speed are excluded from the course by the arbiters of fashion.

The celebrated violinist Ole Bull gave a concert here the other evening, assisted, according to the bills, "by an eminent pianist, a celebrated performer on the cornet, and a distinguished Prima Donna." The latter title was evidently a misnomer; as the lady, in my opinion, was not sufficiently skilled in the art of melody to be entitled to the first place in any opera, unless an Ethiopian burlesque.

Ole himself is in a very good state of preservation, considering that his life has been one of disappointments, reverses, and vicissitudes. He is not likely to hang up his fiddle and his bow for some years to come, unless so ordered by Providence; although I observed that the frosty fingers of Time had been playing with his locks and left their indelible impress.

Montgomery has more the air and appearance of a New York town than any Southern city that I have yet visited. Notwithstanding its Northern aspect, most of the inhabitants are ultra Southerners, who adhere with tenacity to their "peculiar institutions." The legislature not being in session, I have not had an opportunity to see much of the office-holding and office-seeking chivalry. Many of the guests of our hotel appear to be members of the legal profession; at least, so I judged from their attachment to the *bar*-room, which is the best patronized part of the house. Its patrons, however, do not all seem to be professional men; but planters, cotton-brokers, and others without any particular business or occupation. The topic most frequently discussed is cotton, and "niggers," which being rather a dry subject, those engaged in it were often obliged to resort to the bar, to lubricate their vocal organs, so that they may be understood by those around them.

Montgomery has become a great mart for cotton. Nearly all that is grown in Central Alabama is brought to this city to be shipped down the river, which flows for more than four hundred miles through the richest cotton region of the South, and carries each year thousands of bales of this valuable commodity to Mobile and New Orleans. Cotton is in reality the circulating blood which gives vitality to the state. All classes are interested in its culture, from the princely merchant to the lowly artisan; the wealthy planter with his broad fields and army of slaves, as well as the humble occupant of a cabin with a few contiguous acres. A failure of the cotton crop would cast a gloom over the entire community. It would paralyze their internal commerce, create a panic in their monetary affairs, and be absolutely ruinous to all planters of small means. Negroes, unlike their masters, are never affected by the price of cotton. Sometimes their market value is slightly diminished by a failure of the crop, or increased somewhat by an abundant harvest; yet they, as a class, are generally indifferent to its fluctuations. If they are not over-tasked or abused, and have a sufficiency of creature comforts, they appear to be satisfied and happy.

I find that the cost of living at the South, especially in cities and large towns, is considerably greater than at the North. I was told by a wealthy resident of this city that it would be cheaper for him to board with his entire family—some eight or ten in number—at any of the first-class hotels in New York, than to keep house here, notwithstanding he owned all his family servants and the dwelling he occupied. Most kinds of food, with the exception of those Southern *staples*, "hog and hominy," are very dear, and the supply is not always equal to the demand. At least I have found it so in several cases when my appetite has been sharpened by travel. Many of their luxuries are brought from the North, but frequently, when they reach their place of destination, they no longer deserve the name, time and the climate having so impaired their edible qualities as to render them only fit to be used in the manufacture of bacon.

The keeping of so many slaves about their dwellings is an important item in the expense of living. Not that the food they eat and the clothes they wear, cost so very much; but they are idle, careless, and destructive, and wasteful to excess. In the culinary department, every article of food, whether prepared or in a crude state, has to be kept under lock and key; and when wanted for use, weighed or measured out, or it will be wasted or dispensed with ruinous prodigality. I have observed, in passing some of their first-class residences, the yard literally swarming with these human chattels; frequently a dozen or more in sight, of both sexes, and comprising at least three generations. Of that number, perhaps not more than two or three were of any service to their owner; the rest being incapacitated for work, by youth, infirmity, or age. I have no doubt that two or three domestics of the Teutonic or Celtic race, at a cost of as many hundred dollars per annum, will do more work, and with much less waste, than a whole family of slaves, whose yearly keeping and *wasting* cannot be accounted less than from eight to twelve hundred dollars.

Slave labor undoubtedly is profitable to the owners or occupants of large inland plantations, away from cities and towns, where the able-bodied of both sexes are made available as field hands. But here, as well as in other populous places at the South, where they are mainly employed as house servants, or in taking care of the premises of their owners, the labor of the few hardly compensates for the cost of maintaining the many. This class of servants are allowed more liberties than plantation negroes; of these they take advantage, and shirk labor whenever they can.

To a Northerner imbued with republican principles and inheriting the sentiments and prejudices of his Puritan ancestors, the existence of slavery, in its most favorable form, must appear unnatural and forbidding. But a few months' residence at the South will, I opine, so change his views and soften his prejudices that he will regard the system with less abhorrence. I am no friend to slavery in the abstract, neither do I admire the practical workings of the system, as it is not in accordance with my views of equal-rights and universal freedom. Yet from observations made during a two months' residence at the South, I am convinced that the slaves, as a class, are not so badly off as many of us suppose. They are generally well treated, and enjoy as many, if not more physical comforts than a majority of the free negroes at the North; and I am inclined to believe that *the masters are, on the whole, more to be pitied than the slaves themselves.*

The laws of Cuba are more favorable to emancipation, and protect the negro far better than do ours. The slaves on that island, according to the Code, must be worked only a specified number of hours each day, and their masters are obliged to provide them with a permanent subsistence. On Sundays and holidays they are allowed to work in their own gardens, or employ their time as they choose. Being by law protected in the enjoyment of a certain amount of property, they can, if disposed, apply their earnings to the purchase of their own freedom. The value of a slave, which is established by arbitration, in no case exceeds five hundred dollars, although his market value may be considerably more; and as soon as he has accumulated fifty dollars, his master is obliged to accept it towards the purchase of his freedom. Every instalment thus made secures for the slave a proportionate control of his own time, and it is not uncommon to see slaves who have three or four days in the week at their disposal. In case he should be sold before the expiration of his bondage, the amount he has paid must be carried to his credit by the new owner. A slave may also have the benefit of a change of masters provided he can show that he has been ill used. If, however, he can find some one willing to become his purchaser, and the parties cannot agree upon his value, they go before a commissioner appointed by government, who fixes a price, which the owner is obliged to accept, and in return make out a bill of sale to the new purchaser. The negro may have so bad a reputation that he cannot find any one willing to buy him. In that event, he remains with his master, who having taken him for *worse* instead of *better*, as the ladies sometimes take their husbands, is obliged to feed, clothe, and take care of him during sickness and health, in decrepitude and age. But the slaves in Cuba are regarded by their owners more as chattels than human beings, and there exists none of that affectionate regard so often manifested between master and servant in the Southern States. The slaves here, as a class, are more contented and happy, and apparently much better off than most of the emancipated negroes. The free negroes of the South, to speak paradoxically, are not in reality as free as the slaves themselves, and are apparently less happy and contented. Even the African in his bondage feels his own superiority, and looks the very picture of contemptuous pity as he exclaims—"He, poor miserable nigger, has no massa to take care of him."

Among the many objectionable features in the institution of slavery, the separation of families and the sundering of conjugal ties have always appeared to me the most odious and inhuman. I find, on inquiry, that this is seldom practiced—at least, not to very great extent; and from the slaves themselves, I learn that this separation, when it does exist, is not generally regarded by them as a very great affliction.

I had a conversation a few days ago with an unctuous specimen of *Ham*-anity by the name of "Nick," who was as black as his Satanic namesake, but of fewer evil propensities, if there is any truth in physiognomy, I asked him his age.

"Thirty seben nighabouts, Massa!" said he, respectfully touching his hat.

"Are you married, Nick?"

"Yas, Massa, I spose I is!"

"How many children have you?"

"Wall, I spects I'm de fader of ten, yaw, yaw."

Here he displayed a set of teeth that would have excited the envy of many a Northern belle.

"Ten children? Why, Nick, that is quite a family for so young a man as you!"

"Why yas, Massa, Ise some on children!"

"How old is your wife?"

"Do-no zackly, but reckon she be some younger dan me!"

"Is she stout and healthy?"

"She be all dat, massa!"

"Does she belong to your master?"

"No, her massa lives a heap ways from here!"

"How often do you go to see her?"

"Do-no zacklv, sometimes once a month, and some-times nary as often!"

"Wouldn't you like to see your wife and children more frequently?"

"I do-no, sar, sometimes I tink I would, but massa says I go dare nuff, and he knows better dan me."

This conversation occurred nearly as I have related it, and is a fair specimen of the stolidity and indifference of the negroes on most of the Southern plantations. I refer to the genuine, full-blooded African, before his admixture with the gentle blood of the chivalric South, for, to use a sporting phrase, "blood will tell," whether it be in the horses of the North, or in the colored chattels of the South. It is some-thing that will reveal itself whether in man or beast. But a truce to this nonsense, this dark rendering of a *dark* subject.

I came to this city contemplating a trip down the Alabama River to Mobile, and from there to New Orleans, but the weather is becoming so hot that I almost fear, in my present state of health, to risk a visit to those "infected districts," or to trust myself for three or four days on a crowded steamer, with indifferent accommodations. If I abandon this trip, I shall seek a more invigorating climate. My next letter will probably be from New Orleans or Nashville. ******

24

James Stirling

February 1857

JAMES STIRLING (1805–1883), a Scot, generally presented commonplace ideas of the time. For example, he took a purely materialistic view of the conditions of slaves. Consequently, he divided slaves into field hands, whose physical existence was the most miserable, especially on large plantations with overseers; house servants, whose work was lighter and who were constantly with their white owners; and the slaves of small farmers, whose physical existence differed little from their masters. Stirling overlooked the psychological and spiritual aspect of race slavery. His comments were, however, based on interviews of plantation owners and former slaves.

James Stirling, *Letters from the Slave States* (London: John W. Parker and Son,1857), 163–162 and 178–180.

MONTGOMERY, ALABAMA, 2nd February, 1857.

Olmsted gives a very poor account of his fellow-passengers on the Alabama river. He says they were 'a rough, coarse style of people, drinking a great deal'—'very profane'—'often showing the handles of concealed weapons about their persons;'—and gambling during the whole passage, night and day, except on Sunday. My experience of Alabama river life was very different. The passengers seemed a very quiet, respectable class of people. There was no swearing or profanity to be heard, and no gambling to be seen. The only appearance of intemperance I noticed was in the case of a genteel-looking young man, who came on board at Mobile in a state of intoxication. I allude to this contrast, not only because it shows how careful a traveller should be in drawing general inferences from his partial

"Scene on the Alabama River, Loading Cotton" from **Ballou's Pictorial Drawing-Room Companion,** *28 November 1857.*

experience, but because it illustrates the different waves of population that surge up and down this country. Mr. Olmsted's fellow-passengers, he says, 'were generally cotton-planters going to Mobile on business, or emigrants bound to Texas or Arkansas.' Those who ascended the Alabama with me were mostly, I understood, business-men from New Orleans or Mobile, going north to make their Spring purchases, or Northern men returning from a business tour to the South. In manner they were a little reserved, but perfectly gentlemanly, and it gives me pleasure to be able to qualify so far the severe judgment of an American observer.

. . . The towns, and even cities, which I have seen in the South, are ill-paved, and utterly in want of sewerage. New Orleans has nothing but open gutters to carry off its putrescent waters, and this in the City of the Plague *par excellence* . . . The streets of Montgomery, Columbus, and Macon, are unpaved, not even planked; and the sewerage consists of huge ditches cut in the sand at each side of the streets, or down the middle. The absence of stone is some excuse for the want of paving; but why can the Southerners not have plank causeways and pavements as well as Northerners and Canadians! Surely they have pine enough! Yes, they have pine enough, but they lack that high spirit of civilization which is the soul of the North and of Western Canada. What capital they save, and that is not much, they lay out in niggers. Niggers and cotton—cotton and niggers; these are the law and the prophets to the men of the South.

Another criterion of civilization is roads. Judged by its roads, the South is far behind. In Kentucky I saw some good roads. In Tennessee they have some "pikes" (turnpike-roads), and some "mud-roads." In Louisiana, Alabama, and Georgia, I have as yet met no well-made road. In the town of Montgomery I saw a country wagon with six mules, and the spokes of the wheels plastered over up to the very naves with thick tenacious mud. And Montgomery is the capital of the State!

25

William Kingsford

December 1857

William Kingsford (1819–1898) is assumed to be the author of *Impressions*, which was published anonymously, first as letters in a Toronto newspaper. Born in London, Kingsford first went to Canada in 1837 as a private in the dragoon guards, where he participated in quelling a rebellion and then terrorizing the patriot party. He was a well-built six-footer who always relished the active life. When the fighting was over, the cavalry lost its attraction, and he refused the offer of a commission by his colonel. In military service, he had learned surveying and began his career as a civil engineer as Montreal's city surveyor. Subsequently, he worked in various engineering positions in Canada, New York, and Panama. By 1865, he had returned to England and used his fluency in French, German, Italian, and Spanish to facilitate his advice on railroad construction on the Continent. In 1867, he returned to Canada where he continued to work in railroad engineering—sometimes in an official government patronage position (when the conservatives were in power) and other times as a freelance engineer and consultant. In 1879, he was finally dismissed from government service, partially because of patronage and partly because professionalism was replacing the old amateurism.

Kingsford wrote most of his adult life. In 1844, he founded the *Montreal Times*, a very conservative periodical. In fact, he participated as a vigilante in the election riots of 1844, leading the conservatives to take control of a polling station. Two years later, reform party adversaries took their revenge, almost killing Kingsford. He wrote political commentary for several newspapers, and served as Canadian correspondent for a London newspaper. He wrote about engineering, and he even wrote theater and music reviews. In 1879, his engineering career effectively over, he began writing on Canadian history, completing his ten-volume *History of Canada* in 1898. Although it was received with public acclaim in both Canada and England, he again ran afoul of growing professionalism. The academic historians criticize his history for a number of faults. These faults—conventional commonplaces, uninspiring prose, and digressions—can be applied to *Impressions*. Kingsford, who loved the active life and was devoted to building the British Empire in Canada, was not one to appreciate subtleties, or even notice them.

Kingsford, who lived the life of a self-taught amateur when professionalism and specialization were beginning to prevail, was a founder of the Canadian Society of Civil Engineers and a fellow of the Royal Society of Canada.

William Kingsford, *Impressions of the West and South During a Six Weeks' Holiday* (Toronto: A. H. Armour and Co., 1858, 66–72.

I drove over Mobile, and felt like Goethe's friend Beirich, that so far as it went, after all one's experience there was in reality nothing to experience, and made my preparations for starting, having determined to take the land route. By it you do not pass up the Alabama river, but you enter one of its forks—the Tansaw which runs parallel to the former, some six miles or so from it—the two embonchures being but a trifling distance apart. It is a winding stream through a flat country, in some parts narrow, with alligator swamps on each side, but beyond the reeds and rushes there is a rich foliage. The season was not opportune, to meet any of these not too graceful saurians, but some twenty miles up we did see a small fellow, of some three or four feet long swimming inshore, which could hardly have been expected, for the day was cold and raw. In summer, I am told they are plentiful enough, and as all sportsmen wage unrelenting war against them, no few of them are shot. About five we arrived at Stockton, where we saw the stages ready for us, and I soon learned that I was the only passenger. On the boat there were but four passengers, and two of them left us at the first miserable landing to take the stage for Florida, while the third came on to Stockton. It is a place of about nine houses, yet its name is on the map, and one would imagine by seeing it there, that it was a thriving and bustling town. Generally, however, there is but little travel in this direction, and the route is maintained purely as a mail route. Even we may wonder what sustains the small village. I could learn nothing beyond that the stage company had stables there, and indeed every twenty miles of the distance to Montgomery there are similar establishments for the horses; otherwise it is almost a wilderness. The main route is by the Alabama river from Mobile to Montgomery, and when there is plenty of water in the stream, the first class boats make the trip in about three days, the distance three hundred and forty miles, being in no small degree increased by the undulations of the river. In seasons when the water is low there is great risk of detention. The mail, however, is bound by contract to make the distance in 40 hours to connect with the Railways running east, so at least 48 hours are saved by the land route which runs traversely in a direct line between the two points. A Railway is now being constructed from Montgomery, some twenty-five miles of which are in operation towards Pensacola, and possibly a branch may be carried to a point opposite Mobile. Evidently such a scheme would insure all the travel between New Orleans and Washington; but there is difficulty in getting the stock taken up. The design for the present is to construct only the main line, and by all accounts to do so will be no easy task, for the country is but poorly settled. I sat on the box with the driver of one of the stages who was very intelligent; and as we started about six or so, I thought it would be no great harm to enquire where we could get some supper. I learned, however, that it was a meal not in fashion on the western part of the road, for the proprietor of the establishment, finding that there were no travellers to eat supper, had retired from the business. I enquired accordingly if something could not be had where we changed horses, which would be about ten, the distance being twenty miles; but I learned that the horse-keepers boarded some two miles from the stable, and the driver added that where he himself stopped, it would be equally impossible; however he was good enough to tell me, that he would divide what he had brought for himself. Fortunately I had something which I could add towards the supper, so we did the best we could with cold broiled fish and some biscuits. It now came on to rain, so I retired from my seat to the monotony of the inside; and certainly although the rain poured in torrents, and the roads were as bad as they could be, no time was lost. As I had been told, there was evidently no doubt but that I would arrive at the hour named, for no obstacle seemed to retard the driver, and we dashed along without the least regard either to the roughness or bad condition of the road. I was not sorry to see daylight, for it was a dreary ride that wet night, besides it gave promise of breakfast, which came in due time. The rain had now passed over and I took my old seat, but my benevolent friend who had shared his supper with me was not there. I must confess that I was disappointed in the appearance of the forest trees. Compared to a Canadian wood scene they were insignificant. Nothing was there equal to our noble pines, if we except the magnolia and the evergreen oak. Both, however, were of rare occurrence. There is the well known Georgia pine, but it is by no means so fine a tree as its northern brother, and generally the timber has, what one of our lumberers would call a dwarfish look. As we approached Montgomery the country becomes more settled, and we took dinner at a farm house which had some pretensons to comfort. Small settlements succeed each other, but generally the buildings had a delapidated look, and there was an air of poverty over the whole route. Now and then, in new northern settlements we come to spots where city comforts are unknown, and those who dwell in towns know nothing of the hardships which early settlers undergo. But in these cases, although the house is merely a log hut, and there is but one room in it, you never meet misery and squalor. Rather, if you put out of mind the blessings of pavements and gas lights, and the cheerful association with cultivated and genial minds, a few weeks not only will reconcile you to the life, but the free air of the forest will give you a sense of independence and manhood which leads you to deem the obstacles before you but slight. No man lives in communion with nature in vain, unless depressing cares bear him down in his own despite. But as I passed by these places, there was a weary spirit-broken look about them, which impressed me that those whose days were cast in this spot hoped for no change—that they had accepted their

"View of the Capitol, Montgomery, Alabama" from **Ballou's Pictorial Drawing-Room Companion,** *21 November 1857. View up Market Street (today's Dexter Avenue) from the artesian basin to the Capitol. Artist: Kilburn.*

destiny—and I could not but ask myself—is this a consequence of slavery? For to my mind it is the white man placed in indifferent circumstances in the south, who deserves the sympathy of his race. As we advanced the road became worse. It has been my lot to pass over many roads—on shanty roads—roads cut for the first time through bush land, which ran round every tree—on mule tracks—on broken plank roads—on paths unpassable half the year—but I do not think that there is such a road in existence as the last thirty miles of this route. So long as we were on the sandy soil of the high land, spots here and there were only objectionable; but we had descended to a lower level where the soil was of clay. It was now quite dark and raining fast. Literally—one more passenger had now joined us—we had to make a purchase with our legs and back to prevent us being pitched up to the roof of the stage. But on the drivers went, the time had to be made, or a heavy forfeit paid. One of the reasons why the road is in such a bad condition is, that the railway was near completion, and, perhaps, before this letter is in type, the engine will pass over half of the distance. But the night I was there, I may pronounce it to be the worst road that I ever saw, heard, or dreamed off. It turned, too, quite cold, and when we stopped at a plantation where supper was prepared, and where we were to take the railway in the morning for Montgomery, I felt as if I was leaving purgatory. We were unusually late on arriving; indeed, they had been looking out for us two hours. Hence we had many apologies for our half-cold meal, but there was a blazing fire, and there were beds on which we could sleep for an hour, such was the time allotted. So we sat down while the poor sleepy negroes ran round us to supply our wants, which fortunately were moderate enough. At the time appointed the stage came to drive us one more mile to meet the railway, and we sat for about half an hour in the grey of the morning until the cars came up. In them we eagerly took our seats, knowing that for the next two hours we were safe from such inflictions as we had been subjected to, and without further difficulty we came into Montgomery.

The last named city on the Alabama River, is the capital of the State. It is not marked by any peculiarity. The capital stands prominently on high ground, and there is nothing to note, as differing from other cities of its size. There are two artesian wells, which supply the city with water, and the basins stand in the public streets, perfectly easy of access. It was Sunday when I arrived, so I had to wait for the train at five. The main streets in the afternoon were thronged with the negro population, who are generally slaves, for I learned that there are very few free blacks in the State. There are two routes which lead to Charleston, and there is little choice between them. But I was determined by the desire to pass over the Macon and Millen route, the scene of that extraordinary series of duels, the account of which found its way in the London *Times*. I, therefore, chose the southern route, by Columbus to Macon. Being composed of many lines, we change cars sufficiently often, but the connection being made by omnibuses, the annoyance is but trifling, for the baggage is checked through, and the extent of your labor is to pass from one coach seat to another. On starting, the train was composed of two parts, and according to your destination you took your seat. At Opalika, some seventy miles from Montgomery, one set of cars was borne away north to Atalanta, while the remainder was taken on to Columbus. Certainly despatch is not an element in the management of Southern Railways, and it seemed strange to me, whose Railway education, such as it is, had taught, that not a second should be wasted, to see the engine of the passenger train shunting cars at stations with as much deliberation, as if to do so constituted its whole duty. But the time table gives only about fifteen miles an hour, and hence in some instances we delayed twenty and thirty minutes at a station. We arrived in Columbus by night, and were driven through the City to take the Macon Road. At Macon there is an excellent station where the lines meet, and there are all the conditions of comfort in the shape of a good hotel, in the building.

26

Charles Mackay

March 1858

CHARLES MACKAY (1812–1889), much admired in his own day, thought of himself as a poet. Although not formally educated, he was proficient in French, German, Italian, and Spanish, as well as being a self-taught authority on Celtic—he was a native Scot—and a prolific writer in a variety of fields. For example, by thirty, he had published a novel, three volumes of essays, three volumes of poetry, a history of London, a guide to the River Thames, and many popular songs. His creative work was, however, mediocre, though popular. Politically, "the Poet of the People," was a Liberal, contributing to and editing several Scottish and English Liberal periodicals in which he spoke for the working man, advocating democracy, equality, self-help, and temperance. He was a Celtic nationalist, of sorts, writing on the Celtic language in both English and French.

In 1857 and 1858, Mackay toured the United States and Canada lecturing on "Songs National, Historical, and Popular," as well as meeting with national figures, including contemporary luminaries such as Emerson, Holmes, Longfellow, and Prescott.

Mackay returned to the United States from early 1862 to late 1865 to serve as the New York correspondent for the London *Times*. He associated with important people, met Lincoln—and later, at the end of the decade, escorted Jefferson Davis on a tour of the Scottish highlands.

Charles Mackay, *Life and Liberty in America: or, Sketches of a Tour in the*

United States and Canada in 1857–8, (New York: Harper & Brothers, Publishers, 1859), 185–186.

Montgomery is capital of the State of Alabama, and carries on a considerable business in the forwarding of cotton and other produce to Mobile. Its population is under 10,000. It offers nothing to detain the traveler, and has nothing remarkable about it except the badness of its principal hotel. Among the numerous eccentricities of this establishment may be mentioned the fact that it contains no bells in its rooms. By this economy the traveler is compelled, if he want any thing, to go to the top of the stairs and use his lungs, or, if that be disagreeable or unavailing, to help himself, which is, perhaps, his most advisable mode of getting out of the difficulty. Another peculiarity of this remarkable hostelry is (or was) that nothing is (or was) to be had on a Sunday evening after six o'clock. Having dined by compulsion of the custom of the place at one o'clock, I sought out a negro waiter about nine o'clock, and asked for some refreshment. There was nothing to be had—no tea, no milk, no meat, not even a crust of bread. "Is the bar open?" I inquired, with a faint hope that that department might prove more hospitable, and afford a hungry traveler a "cracker" (the American name for a biscuit, and for a Southern rustic) and a glass of beer or wine. The hope was vain; the bar-keeper had shut up at six o'clock. It was a case of starvation in a land of plenty; and, to make the matter more provoking, it was starvation charged in the bill at the rate of two dollars and a half per diem. I made a friend of the negro, however, and he borrowed a crust of bread for me out of doors somewhere, and managed to procure me a lump or two of sugar; a worthy Scotchman at Mobile had, when I left that city, filled me a pocket-flask with genuine

from the "Old Country;" and, with these abundant resources, and a tea-kettle, I was enabled to be independent of the landlord of the bell-less, comfortless, foodless hotel of Montgomery, Alabama.

27

Thomas Low Nichols

March 1859

Thomas Low Nichols (1815–1901), a native of New Hampshire, became an advocate of some of the more unusual fads and fashions of the nineteenth century, as well as legitimate health issues such as exercise, second-hand smoke, fatty diets, and good hygiene. After leaving Dartmouth Medical College in 1834 without taking a degree, he worked as a journalist for a number of years. By 1840, he was writing both fiction and nonfiction in New York City. There he read some of the utopian socialists and developed an interest in communal living. Combining these interests with those of his wife, Mary Gove, a hydrotherapist and popular health lecturer, he opened a water-cure house in New York that relied on a variety of cures, including vegetarianism. His advocacy of free love, often misinterpreted as advocating promiscuity, resulted in his having to found his own journal to get his ideas published. After graduating from the University of the City of New York with a medical degree, Dr. Nichols and his wife founded the first hydropathic medical school in the United States. The Nicholses then pursued spiritualism, but on conversion to Roman Catholicism in 1857, renounced all their writings that were contrary to Church teachings.

The restrictions of the Civil War, and his published writings regarding free love and assertions that Southern slaves were physically better off than laboring classes elsewhere, prompted the Nicholses to emigrate to England, where they opened a water-cure house and a vegetarian restaurant and supported themselves by journalism and writing fiction, attacking alcohol, capital punishment, and conscription.

Thomas L. Nichols, *Forty Years of American Life, 1821–1861*, 2 vols. (London: John Maxwell and Company, 1864), I: 228–238.

CHAPTER XIX.

UP THE ALABAMA.

. . . It was a soft, bright, warm evening in March (which corresponds to the June of this colder clime) when I took my way down the broad streets of Mobile, bound up the Mobile and Alabama rivers to Montgomery, the beautiful capital of the state, and, for a time, of the Southern Confederacy. [Compiled in London after the Civil War had begun.]

As I approached the pier, the air was filled with the music of a steam organ on one of the boats, which was played by a German musical artist, engaged by the year, at a handsome salary. It is a strange music that fills the air with a vast body of harmony, carrying with it the impression of the power that gives it birth—in the range of long cylindrical boilers—of which the organ is the melodious collection of escape pipes and safety valves. Some are played by machinery, like street barrel-organs. This had a fingerboard and organist.

The Mobile river, which is but an extension of the deep bay into which flow the Tombigbee and the Alabama, is broad and deep, and was now bank full. There were scarcely any visible shores. We steamed through a vast forest, which opened before us in picturesque reaches of the richest semi-tropical foliage, and the air was thick with the odour of the orange-blossom and the jessamine. The two fine rivers which unite to form the Mobile, have, like it, preserved their Indian names, but how the tribe that found for two of them such musical designations as Mobile and Alabama ever came to name a river the Tombigbee, I shall leave to some Choctaw or Cherokee to find a satisfactory explanation. Perhaps I do the aboriginal savages injustice. The Americans are not slow at corrupting names when they can make them sound more familiar. This very word, Tombigbee, if I mistake not, is a corruption of an Indian word, which it resembles in sound; the word signifying a blow-gun. The Southern steamer, "Bueneta," was known by the steamboat men as "the Bone-eater;" just as asparagus is popularly known as "sparrow-grass." In the early times all names had meanings.

The captain of our steamer was an Irishman—tall, handsome, eloquent, and thoroughly and enthusiastically Southern American in his views and feelings. For twenty years he had steamed up and down the Alabama, and he could not have been more devoted to his adopted country, or the section to which he belonged, had he been born upon the banks of the river.

As we sat forward of the pilot-house, on the promenade deck, enjoying the soft and perfume-laden evening breeze, he told me his story. When a boy of nineteen, he found himself, a raw immigrant, with five dollars in his pocket, on the banks of this river, looking for work; and the first, hardest, and roughest he could find was that of a deck-hand on a steamboat. He became one of a gang of white and black, who stood ready to land and receive freight, take in wood, and feed the furnaces. This hard and rapid work came at all hours of day or night, and the fare was as hard as the work. I have seen the men, a group of negroes on one side of the boat, and of the white hands, mostly Irish or Germans, on the other, eating their bread and bacon, and drinking black coffee from an iron pan, seated on piles of wood or bales of cotton.

But the wages, to a poor Irish boy, were a strong inducement. They gave him eight pounds a month, and found, in a rough fashion; bacon for food, and for his bed a dry goods-box or cotton-bale. He went to work, and was so sober, active, and intelligent, that the mate had no excuse to knock him into the river with a billet of wood, as was the custom with some of them.

He had been a week on the boat, when, one dark night, a fire was seen, and a shout heard, on the bank of the river. The mate would not land at the inconvenient place, but sent Patrick ashore in the yawl. Standing by the signal fire at the river-side, attended by two or three grinning negroes, was a planter, who handed him a package, and said, "Here is thirty-four thousand dollars. Give it to the captain or clerk, and ask him to deposit it for me in the Planters' bank, as soon as you get in. Tell them not to forget it, as it is to pay a note that falls due day after to-morrow."

Patrick put the money into his bosom, and pushed off into the dark and lonely river. Doubtless he might have got ashore, and away; and doubtless he thought of it, as he felt the fortune in his bosom; but he pulled straight for the boat, as she lay, blowing off steam in mid channel. And while he rowed he thought of what he must do when he should get on board.

"What was it all about?" asked the mate, as he sprang on the low deck.

"A message for the captain, sir," said Patrick.

"Then go into the cabin and give it to him, and be quick about it," said the not over-polite officer.

Patrick went up the companion way to the cabin, on the second deck, where he found the jolly captain, with a group of planters and merchants, busy at a game of poker, and more busy with the punch. He turned to the clerk, who was deeper in both punch and poker than the captain.

"Faith, an' this will never do," said Patrick. "If I give them the money to-night, they will lose it at poker, and never remember it in the morning." So he went forward on deck again, and stowed the package of bank-notes at the bottom of his clothes-bag in the forecastle, if so small a hole can be dignified by such an appellation.

In the morning, when the officers were awake and sober, Patrick handed over his money and message.

"What is all this?" said the captain; "where did you get this money?"

"I went ashore in the yawl for it last night, sir."

"And why did you not bring it to the office at once?"

"I did, sir; but you and the clerk were both very busy."

The passengers, who had been engaged in the same line of business, had a hearty laugh.

"Young man," said the captain, "how long have you been on this boat?"

"A week, sir."

"And how much money have you got?"

"Five dollars, sir."

"Very well—go to your work."

In three weeks Patrick was second mate; in a year, first mate; and not long after, captain; and now, as we sat talking on the Alabama, he had a wife, children, a plantation, and two or three steamboats; and thought Alabama the greatest state, and Mobile the most promising city in the world.

The Alabama flows through one of the richest cotton countries in America. It winds about as if it had taken a contract to water or drain as much of the State as possible, and give a good steamboat landing to every plantation. Our general course from Mobile to Montgomery was north-east, but we were often steaming for hours south-west, and in every other direction. The distance, as the crow flies, is a hundred and sixty miles; by the river it is little less than four hundred. The banks of the river are low in some places; in others high and precipitous, and everywhere covered with the richest and most luxuriant vegetation. There were a thousand landscapes in which a painter would revel.

The passengers were a curious study for the traveller. Here was a swarthy planter, taking his newly-purchased gang of hands up to his newly-bought plantation. He had purchased a thousand acres of wild land for twenty-five thousand dollars—five thousand down. He had bought four or five families of negroes at New Orleans, twenty-five thousand more—half cash. And now he was ready to clear away the forest, and raise cotton; to buy more negroes, to raise more cotton, to buy more negroes, to raise more cotton; and so on, until tired of the monotonous accumulation.

There were Virginians, also, who had been spending the winter in New Orleans, and were now returning before the hot season should commence. They were attended by their body servants; and nicer, better behaved, more intelligent, gentlemanly and ladylike people of colour it would be difficult to find anywhere. If there is such a thing as genius for service or servitude, it is developed in these "hereditary bondsmen," who care so little to "be free," that they will not "strike the blow," even when urgently invited to do so.

We had politicians and preachers, and three Sisters of Charity from the hospitals of New Orleans, going home to recruit, a thousand miles to their mother house in Maryland. All over the South these Sisters travel free. Where there is yellow fever they have friends, and no Southerner would touch their money.

We stopped at Selma long enough for a ramble through its broad and shaded streets. It is built in too grand and ambitious a style, but its export of cotton is so large, that the money must be spent in some way, so they build great blocks of six-storey houses. The town is watered by artesian wells of great depth, which throw up an abundant supply.

At last we are at Montgomery. It is a beautiful little town, of ten thousand inhabitants, built upon more hills than Rome, with deeper valleys between them. It is a city of palaces and gardens; not crowded into a narrow space, but spread out broadly over the hills and valleys, with wide streets, handsome villas, elegant shops, and such gardens as only the South, with its glorious wealth of foliage and flowers, can give. A large and handsome domed state-house crowns one of the finest eminences.

Montgomery impresses the traveller with its beauty and riches. It is the centre of one of the finest cotton regions, in the finest cotton state—a state of sixty thousand square miles—and the plantations, which stretch away on every side, were in the highest state of cultivation. Every negro could make five or six bales of cotton, besides raising his own corn and bacon. A hundred negroes, therefore, besides their own support, made five or six hundred bales of cotton, worth twenty-five or thirty thousand dollars, which represents the clear profit of a well-conducted plantation. The yearly export of the single town of Montgomery was 106,000 bales, amounting to 5,300,000 dollars a-year. Well might it be prosperous and rich. There may have been poor people, but I saw none. In a thousand miles of that country one never sees a hand held out for charity. On every side is abounding wealth. The population of such a city is like nothing in Europe. The middle class is small—the lower class is wanting. There is more wealth, style, and fashion in a town like Montgomery, of ten thousand inhabitants, than in a European town of eighty or a hundred thousand.

When I arrived in Montgomery, the good citizens had a new sensation. Since the abolition of the slave trade, no negroes had ever been imported from Africa, until the owner of the yacht *Wanderer* took a fancy to buy a small cargo at Dahomy, and distribute them as an experiment among the planters of Alabama. They did not sell for much; as there was risk in the purchase, few cared to try them. There was one native African boy at Montgomery; a bright little fellow enough, a pet with his master, of whom he had become very fond, and the little savage was learning the language, manners, and customs very rapidly. There was no need to punish him. It was only necessary to threaten to send him back to Dahomy. He would fall on his knees in great distress, and earnestly beg to be saved from so terrible a misfortune.

It is sometimes represented in English papers that negroes have been smuggled into the Southern States, since the African slave trade was abolished in 1808. The small cargo of the yacht *Wanderer* was the only one I ever heard of. The planters, I believe, do not wish to depreciate the money valuation of their negroes by importation from Africa, and they do not want the trouble of training savages, when they have a race already well advanced in its enforced pupilage to civilization. The slave traders of New York and Boston sell their negroes in Cuba or Brazil, when they have the luck to sell them. When the negroes have the good fortune to be rescued from slavery by British cruisers, they are taken to the West Indies or British Guiana, and parcelled out to the planters as apprentices, to become, it is hoped, in due time, free citizens and loyal British subjects, who can have apprentices of their own in the same fashion.

During my visit to Montgomery I made several excursions into the surrounding country and among the plantations. It was in the early spring, and the fields were being ploughed for the cotton planting. The ploughing was mostly done by the mules and women. They took it very easy. I could not see that they hurried to the fields or in the fields. The overseer planned and directed the work. He rode from field to field, when it was going on, and saw, no doubt, that the men with their hoes, and the women, driving the mules, or guiding the ploughs, did their work properly. He had a whip, useful, no doubt, for man or beast, but I never chanced to see him use it on either. I have no doubt that negroes are whipped like white people—soldiers, sailors, wives, and children—boys at school, and apprentices under hard masters, but I never saw it. I do not doubt that there are Legrees in the Southern States. How can I, after six months reading of London police reports? But if I wished to paint a picture of fat and careless enjoyment, it would be a portrait of a young negress I saw riding afield on her mule, on a plantation in Alabama. Her figure, attitude, expression—all told volumes of a care-free life of easy, saucy, animal enjoyment.

Montgomery, like most of the considerable towns in America, has its cemetery laid out like a park or pleasure-ground, and is becoming filled with ambitious marble monuments. A portion of the ground is set apart for negroes, and they, too, have their gravestones, which record their humble virtues. I was struck by the original form of a marble monument which an honest German had raised to an adopted son who had been drowned in the river. The epitaph was so peculiar that I copied it:—

> Stop as you pass by my grave. Here I, John Schockler, rest my remains. I was born in New Orleans, the 22nd of Nov., 1841; was brought up by good friends; not taking their advice, was drowned in this city in the Alabama river, the 27th of May, 1855. Now I warn all young and old to beware of the dangers of this river. See how I am fixed in this watery grave; I have got but two friends to mourn.

What Montgomery now is, or may be in the future, I know not, but I shall always remember it as a bright, beautiful, elegant, and hospitable city, and worthy, from its refinement and hospitality, of a prosperous and noble destiny.

"City of Montgomery, Alabama" View of Montgomery from the north drawn by a special artist traveling with William Howard Russell, correspondent for The Times *of London and published in* Harper's Weekly, *1 June 1861.*

"The Hon. Jefferson Davis, President-Elect of the New Southern Confederacy, Addressing the Citizens of Montgomery, Ala., from the Balcony of the Exchange Hotel, on the Night of February 16th, 1861, and Previous to His Inauguration," from Frank Leslie's Illustrated Newspaper, *16 March 1861.*

Epilogue

William Howard Russell

May 1861

WILLIAM HOWARD RUSSELL (1820–1907) was born and educated in Ireland. He left Trinity College, Dublin, before taking a degree, yet had a knowledge and appreciation of the classics. At twenty-one he became a correspondent for *The Times* of London. Then Russell read law in London and was called to the bar when he was thirty. However, he returned to journalism, reporting first on the proceedings of the House of Commons and then, from 1854–56, on the Crimean War. Never particularly popular with the generals, he identified with the junior officers and filed inspired reports on the fighting. His exposing incompetent leadership significantly influenced both the British public and parliamentarians, leading to a degree of military reform. Known as Crimean Russell and Balaclava Russell, he was famous, even being given an honorary LLD by Trinity College. Dr. Russell lectured on the war and began to move within aristocratic circles. *The Times* sent him to India, where for more than a year in the late 1850s, he reported on the mutiny; again his reporting led to reforms, specifically to the ending of summary executions.

The Times again sent him to report on a war, this time the American Civil War. He was received by both the Union and Confederate governments as a sort of semi-official envoy of the British government. Although he favored the North and opposed slavery, he was excluded from reporting on the Union army after filing an uncomplimentary—but accurate—description of the Union debacle at First Bull Run/Manassas. He returned to England after slightly more than a year covering the war. Subsequently, he reported on the Austro-Prussian War, the Franco-Prussian War, and the

Anglo-Zulu War. From 1860–1901, he owned and edited the *Army and Navy Gazette*, again promoting reform, as well as technological advances and conscription.

Sociable, charming, entertaining, as well as brave and candid, Russell moved in the highest circles, including marrying an Italian countess and accompanying the prince of Wales to the Near East and India and the duke of Sutherland to Canada and the United States.

Russell was decorated by the British, French, Prussian, Austrian, Turkish, Greek, and Portuguese governments, and he was knighted in 1895. Sir William Russell was memorialized in the crypt of St. Paul's Cathedral as "the first and greatest of War Correspondents." He was not; he was, however, responsible for war correspondency becoming a separate branch of journalism.

The first passage below is from Russell's *Pictures of Southern Life*, published as letters in *The Times* of London shortly after they were written. This account is shorter and more spontaneous than *My Diary North and South* (the second passage below), published in 1863, which is an expanded account that offers the benefit of hindsight.

William Howard Russell, *Pictures of Southern Life, Social, Political, and Military*. (New York: James G. Gregory, 1861), 15–21.

Montgomery is on an undulating plain, and covers ground large enough for a city of 200,000 inhabitants, but its population is only 12,000. Indeed, the politicians here appear to dislike large cities, but the city designers certainly prepare to take them if they come. There is a large negro population, and a considerable number of a color which forces me to doubt the evidence of my senses rather than the statements made to me by some of my friends, that the planters affect the character of parent in their moral relations merely with the negro race. A waiter at the hotel—a tall, handsome young fellow, with the least tinge of color in his cheek, not as dark as the majority of Spaniards or Italians—astonished me in my ignorance to-day when, in reply to a question asked by one of our party, in consequence of a discussion on the point, he informed me he "was a slave." The man, as he said so, looked confused; his manner altered. He had been talking familiarly to us, but the moment he replied, "I am a slave, sir," his loquacity disappeared, and he walked hurriedly and in silence out of the room. The River Alabama, on which the city rests, is a wide, deep stream, now a quarter of a mile in breadth, with a current of four miles an hour. It is navigable to Mobile, upward of 400 miles, and steamers ascend its waters for many miles beyond this into the interior. The country around is well wooded, and is richly cultivated in broad fields of cotton and Indian corn, but the neighborhood is not healthy, and deadly fevers are said to prevail at certain seasons of the year. There is not much animation in the streets, except when "there is a difficulty among the citizens," or in the eternal noise of the hotel steps and bars. I was told this morning by the hotel keeper that I was probably the only person in the house, or about it, who had not loaded revolvers in his pockets, and one is aware occasionally of an unnatural rigidity scarcely attributable to the osseous structure in the persons of those who pass one in the crowded passages.

Monday, May 6.—To-day I visited the capitol, where the Provisional Congress is sitting. On leaving the hotel, which is like a small Willard's, so far as the crowd in the hall is concerned, my attention was attracted to a group of people to whom a man was holding forth in energetic sentences. The day was hot, but I pushed near to the spot, for I like to hear a stump-speech, or to pick up a stray morsel of divinity in the *via sacra* of strange cities, and it appeared as though the speaker was delivering an oration or a sermon. The crowd was small. Three or four idle men in rough, homespun, makeshift uniforms, leaned against the iron rails enclosing a small pond of foul, green-looking water, surrounded by brick-work, which decorates the space in front of the Exchange hotel. The speaker stood on an empty deal packing-case. A man in a cart was listening with a lacklustre eye to the address. Some three or four others, in a sort of vehicle which might either be a hearse or a piano van, had also drawn up for the benefit of the address. Five or six other men, in long black coats and high hats, some whittling sticks, and chewing tobacco, and discharging streams of discolored saliva, completed the group. "N-i-n-e h'hun' nerd and fifty dollars? Only nine h-hun nerd and fifty dollars offered for him!" exclaimed the

"The City of Montgomery, Alabama, showing the State House where the Congress of the Southern Confederacy meets [met] on February 4, 1861," from Harper's Weekly, *February 9, 1861. Printed in* Ballou's Pictorial Drawing-Room Companion, *November 21, 1857.*

man, in the tone of injured dignity, remonstrance and surprise, which can be insinuated by all true auctioneers into the dryest numerical statements. "Will *no one* make any advance on nine hundred and fifty dollars?" A man near me opened his mouth, spat, and said, "twenty-five." "Only nine hundred and seventy-five dollars offered for him. Why, at's radaklous—only nine hundred and seventy-five dollars! Will no one," &c. Beside the orator auctioneer stood a stout young man of five-and-twenty years of age, with a bundle in his hand. He was a muscular fellow, broad-shouldered, narrow flanked, but rather small in stature; he had on a broad, greasy, old wide-awake, a blue jacket, a coarse cotton shirt, loose and rather ragged trowsers, and broken shoes. The expression of his face was heavy and sad, but it was by no means disagreeable, in spite of his thick lips, broad nostrils, and high cheek-bones. On his head was wool instead of hair. I am neither sentimentalist nor black republican, nor negro-worshipper, but I confess the sight caused a strange thrill through my heart. I tried in vain to make myself familiar with the fact that I could, for the sum of $975, become as absolutely the owner of that mass of blood, bones, sinew, flesh, and brains, as of the horse which stood by my side. There was no sophistry which could persuade me the man was not a man—he was, indeed, by no means my brother, but assuredly he was a fellow-creature. I have seen slave markets in the East, but somehow or other the Orientalism of the scene cast a coloring over the nature of the sales there which deprived them of the disagreeable harshness and matter-of-fact character of the transaction before me. For Turk, or Smyrniote, or Egyptian to buy and sell slaves seemed rather suited to the eternal fitness of things than otherwise. The turbaned, shawled, loose-trowsered, pipe-smoking merchants speaking an unknown tongue looked as if they were engaged in a legitimate business. One knew that their slaves would not be condemned to any very hard labor, and that they would be in some sort the inmates of the family, and members of it. Here it grated on my ear to listen to the familiar tones of the English tongue as the medium by which the transfer was effected, and it was painful to see decent-looking men in European garb engaged in the work before me. Perchance these impressions may wear off, for I meet many English people who are the most strenuous advocates of the slave system, although it is true that their perceptions may be quickened to recognize its beauties by their participation in the profits. The negro was sold to one of the bystanders, and walked off with his bundle, God knows where. "Niggers is cheap," was the only remark of the bystanders. I continued my walk up a long, wide, straight street, or more properly, an unpaved sandy road, lined with wooden houses on each side, and with trees by the side of the footpath. The lower of the two stories is generally used as a shop, mostly of the miscellaneous store kind, in which all sorts of articles are to be had if there is any money to pay for them; and, in the present case, if any faith is to be attached to the conspicuous notices in the windows, credit is of no credit, and the only thing that can he accepted in exchange for the goods is "cash." At the end of this long street, on a moderate eminence, stands a whitewashed or painted edifice, with a gaunt, lean portico, supported on lofty lanky pillars, and surmounted by a subdued and dejected-looking little cupola. Passing an unkempt lawn, through a very shabby little gateway in a brick frame, and we ascend a flight of steps into a hall, from which a double staircase conducts us to the vestibule of the chamber. Any thing much more offensive to the eye cannot well be imagined than the floor and stairs. They are stained deeply by tobacco juice, which has left its marks on the white stone steps and on the base of the pillars outside. In the hall which we have entered there are two tables, covered with hams, oranges, bread and fruits, for the refreshment of members and visitors, over which two sable goddesses, in portentous crinoline, preside. The door of the chamber is open, and we are introduced into a lofty, well-lighted and commodious apartment, in which the Congress of the Confederate States holds its deliberations. A gallery runs half round the room, and is half filled with visitors—country cousins, and farmers of cotton and maize, and, haply, seekers of places great or small. A light and low semicircular screen separates the body of the house, where the members sit, from the space under the gallery, which is appropriated to ladies and visitors. The clerk sits at a desk above this table, and on a platform behind him are the desk and chair of the presiding officer or Speaker of the Congress. Over his head hangs the unfailing portrait of Washington, and a small engraving, in a black frame, of a gentleman unknown to me. Seated in the midst of them, at a senator's desk, I was permitted to "assist," in the French sense, at the deliberations of the Congress. Mr. Howell Cobb took the chair, and a white-headed clergyman was called upon to say prayers, which he did, upstanding, with outstretched hands and closed eyes, by the side of the speaker. The prayer was long and sulphureous. One more pregnant with gunpowder I never heard, nor could aught like it have been heard since.

"Pulpit, drum ecclesiastic,
"Was beat with fist instead of stick."

"The Confederate Senate in Open Session at the Capitol, Montgomery, Ala.—Howell Cobb Presiding," from Harper's Weekly, *4 February 1861. Also printed in* Frank Leslie's Illustrated Newspaper, *2 March 1861.*

The reverend gentleman prayed that the Almighty might be pleased to inflict on the arms of the United States such a defeat that it might be the example of signal punishment forever—that this president might be blessed, and the other president might be the other thing—that the gallant, devoted young soldiers who were fighting for their country might not suffer from exposure to the weather or from the bullets of their enemies; and that the base mercenaries who were fighting on the other side might come to sure and swift destruction, and so on.

Are right and wrong mere geographical expressions? The prayer was over at last, and the house proceeded to business. Although each state has several delegates in Congress, it is only entitled to one vote on a strict division. In this way some curious decisions may be arrived at, as the smallest state is equal to the largest, and a majority of the Florida representatives may neutralize a vote of all the Georgia representatives. For example, Georgia has ten delegates; Florida has only three. The vote of Florida, however, is determined by the action of any two of its three representatives, and these two may, on a division, throw the one state vote into the scale against that of Georgia, for which ten members are agreed. The Congress transacts all its business in secret session, and finds it a very agreeable and commendable way of doing it. Thus, to-day, for example, after the presentation of a few unimportant motions and papers, the speaker rapped his desk, and announced that the house would go into secret session, and that all who were not members should leave.

As I was returning to the hotel there was another small crowd at the fountain. Another auctioneer, a fat, flabby, perspiring, puffy man, was trying to sell a negro girl, who stood on the deal box beside him. She was dressed pretty much like a London servant-girl of the lower order out of place, except that her shoes were mere shreds of leather patches, and her bonnet would have scarce passed muster in the New Cut. She, too, had a little bundle in her hand, and looked out at the buyers from a pair of large sad eyes. "Niggers were cheap;" still here was this young woman going for an upset price of $610, but no one would bid, and the auctioneer, after vain attempts to raise the price and excite competition, said, "Not sold to-day, Sally; you may get down."

Tuesday, May 7.—The newspapers contain the text of the declaration of a state of war on the part of President Davis, and of the issue of letters of marque and reprisal, &c. But it may be asked, who will take these letters of marque? Where is the government of Montgomery to find ships? The answer is to be found in the fact that already numerous applications have been received from the shipowners of New England, from the whalers of New Bedford, and from others in the Northern States, for these very letters of marque, accompanied by the highest securities and guaranties! This statement I make on the very highest authority. I leave it to you to deal with the facts.

To-day I proceeded to the Montgomery Downing street and Whitehall, to present myself to the members of the cabinet, and to be introduced to the President of the Confederate States of America. There is no sentry at the doors, and access is free to all, but there are notices on the doors warning visitors that they can only be received during certain hours. The President was engaged with some gentlemen when I was presented to him, but he received me with much kindliness of manner, and, when they had left, entered into conversation with me for some time on general matters. Mr. Davis is a man of slight, sinewy figure, rather over the middle height, and of erect, soldierlike bearing. He is about fifty-five years of age; his features are regular and well-defined, but the face is thin and marked on cheek and brow with many wrinkles, and is rather careworn and haggard. One eye is apparently blind, the other is dark, piercing, and intelligent. He was dressed very plainly, in a light-gray summer suit. In the course of conversation, he gave an order for the Secretary of War to furnish me with a letter as a kind of passport, in case of my falling in with the soldiers of any military posts who might be indisposed to let me pass freely, merely observing that I had been enough within the lines of camps to know what was my duty on such occasions. I subsequently was presented to Mr. Walker, the Secretary of War, who promised to furnish me with the needful documents before I left Montgomery. In his room were General Beauregard and several officers, engaged over plans and maps, apparently in a little council of war, which was, perhaps, not without reference to the intelligence that the United States troops were marching on Norfolk Navy-Yard, and had actually occupied Alexandria. On leaving the Secretary, I proceeded to the room of the Attorney-General, Mr. Benjamin, a very intelligent and able man, whom I found busied in preparations connected with the issue of letters of marque. Every thing in the offices looked like earnest work and business.

On my way back from the State Department, I saw a very fine company of infantry and three field-pieces, with about one hundred and twenty artillerymen, on their march to the railway station for Virginia. The men were all well equipped, but there were no ammunition wagons for the guns, and the transport consisted solely of a few country carts, drawn by poor horses, out of condition. There is no lack of muscle and will among the men. The troops which I see here are quite fit to march and fight as far as their *personnel* is concerned, and there is no people in the world so crazy with military madness. The very children in the streets ape the air of soldiers, carry little flags, and wear cockades as they strut in the highways, and mothers and fathers feed the fever by dressing them up as Zouaves or Chasseurs.

Mrs. Davis had a small levee to-day in right of her position as wife of the President. Several ladies there probably looked forward to the time when their states might secede from the new Confederation, and afford them the pleasure of holding a reception. Why not Presidents of the State of Georgia, or Alabama? Why not King of South Carolina, or Emperor of Florida? Soldiers of fortune, make your game! Gentlemen politicians, the ball is rolling. There is, to be sure, a storm gathering at the North, but it cannot hurt you, and already there are *condottieri* from all parts of the world flocking to your aid, who will eat your Southern beeves the last of all.

One word more as to a fleet. The English owners of several large steamers are already in correspondence with government here for the purchase of their vessels. The intelligence which had reached the government that their commissioners have gone on to Paris is regarded as unfavorable to their claims, and as a proof that as yet England is not disposed to recognize them. It is amusing to hear the tone used on both sides toward Great Britain. Both are most anxious for her countenance and support, although the North blusters rather more about its independence than the South, which professes a warm regard for the mother country. "But," say the North, "if Great Britain recognizes the South, we shall certainly look on it as a declaration of war." "And," say the South, "if Great Britain does not recognize our privateers' flag, we shall regard it as proof of hostility and of alliance with the enemy." The government at Washington seeks to obtain promises from Lord Lyons that our government will not recognize the Southern Confederacy, but at the same time refuses any guaranties in reference to the rights of neutrals. The blockade of the Southern ports would not occasion us any great inconvenience at present, because the cotton-loading season is over; but if it be enforced in October, there is a prospect of very serious and embarrassing questions arising in reference to the rights of neutrals, treaty obligations with the United States government, the trade and commerce of England, and the law of blockade in reference to the distinctions to be drawn between measures of war and means of annoyance.

As I write, the guns in front of the State Department are firing a salute, and each report marks a state of the Confederacy. They are now ten, as Arkansas and Tennessee are now out of the Union.

William Howard Russell, *My Diary North and South*. (New York: Harper & Brothers, Publisher, 1863), 65–73.

The train for Montgomery [from Macon] started at 9:45 A.M., but I had no time to stop and visit them.

It is evident we are approaching the Confederate capital, for the candidates for office begin to show, and I detected a printed testimonial in my room in the hotel. The country, from Macon in Georgia to Montgomery in Alabama, offers no features to interest the traveller which are not common to the districts already described. It is, indeed, more undulating, and somewhat more picturesque, or less unattractive, but, on the whole, there is little to recommend it, except the natural fertility of the soil. The people are rawer, ruder, bigger—there is the same amount of tobacco-chewing and its consequences—and as much swearing or use of expletives. The men are tall, lean, uncouth, but they are not peasants. There are, so far as I have seen, no rustics, no peasantry in America; men dress after the same type, differing only in finer or coarser material; every man would wear, if he could, a black satin waistcoat and a large diamond pin stuck in the front of his shirt, as he certainly has a watch and a gilt or gold chain of some sort or other. The Irish labourer, or the German husbandman is the nearest approach to our Giles Jolter or the Jacques Bonhomme to be found in the States. The mean white affects the style of the large proprietor of slaves or capital as closely as he can; he reads his papers—and, by-the-by, they are becoming smaller and more whitey-brown as we proceed—and takes his drink with the same air—takes up as much room, and speaks a good deal in the same fashion.

The people are all hearty Secessionists here—the Bars and Stars are flying at the road-stations and from the pine-tops, and there are lusty cheers for Jeff Davis and the Southern Confederacy. Troops are flocking

TWO NORTHERN PRESS VIEWS OF THE INAUGURATION OF JEFFERSON DAVIS, Above and Opposite:

"Inauguration of Jefferson Davis, President of the Southern Confederacy, at Montgomery, Ala., the Capital of the Southern Confederacy, on Monday, Feb. 18, 1861," from Frank Leslie's Illustrated Newspaper, *23 March 1861.*

"Inauguration of President Jefferson Davis on the Steps of the Capitol in Montgomery, Alabama." This image captures the audience at prayer just after Howell Cobb, president of the Confederate Senate, has administered the oath of office. Printed in Harper's Weekly, *9 March 1861. An almost identical image, but with the first Confederate flag on a staff to the left of the clock, was printed in* The New-York Illustrated News, *also 9 March 1861.*

towards Virginia from the Southern States in reply to the march of Volunteers from Northern States to Washington; but it is felt that the steps taken by the Federal Government to secure Baltimore have obviated any chance of successfully opposing the "Lincolnites" going through that city. There is a strong disposition on the part of the Southerners to believe they have many friends in the North, and they endeavour to attach a factious character to the actions of the Government by calling the Volunteers and the war party in the North "Lincolnites," "Lincoln's Mercenaries," "Black Republicans," "Abolitionists," and the like. The report of an armistice, now denied by Mr. Seward officially, was for some time current, but it is plain that the South must make good its words, and justify its acts by the sword. General Scott would, it was fondly believed, retire from the United States' army, and either remain neutral or take command under the Confederate flag, but now that it is certain he will not follow any of these courses, he is assailed in the foulest manner by the press and in private conversation. Heaven help the idol of a democracy!

At one of the junctions General Beauregard, attended by Mr. Manning, and others of his staff, got into the car, and tried to elude observation, but the conductors take great pleasure in unearthing distinguished passengers for the public, and the General was called on for a speech by the crowd of idlers. The General hates speech-making, he told me, and he had besides been bored to death at every station by similar demands. But a man must be popular or he is nothing. So, as next best thing, Governor Manning made a speech in the General's name, in which he dwelt on Southern Rights, Sumter, victory, and abolitiondom, and was carried off from the cheers of his auditors by the train in the midst of an unfinished sentence. There were a number of blacks listening to the Governor, who were appreciative.

Towards evening, having thrown out some slight outworks against accidental sallies of my fellow-passengers' saliva, I went to sleep, and woke up at 11 P.M. to hear we were in Montgomery. A very ricketty omnibus took the party to the hotel, which was crowded to excess. The General and his friends had one room to themselves. Three gentlemen and myself were crammed into a filthy room which already contained two strangers, and as there were only three beds in the apartment it was apparent that we were intended to "double up considerably;" but after strenuous efforts, a little bribery and cajoling, we succeeded in procuring mattresses to put on the floor, which was regarded by our neighbours as a proof of miserable aristocratic fastidiousness. Had it not been for the flies, the fleas would have been intolerable, but one nuisance neutralised the other. Then, as to food—nothing could be had in the hotel—but one of the waiters led us to a restaurant, where we selected from a choice bill of fare, which contained, I think, as many odd dishes as ever I saw, some unknown fishes, oyster-plants, 'possums, racoons, frogs, and other delicacies, and, eschewing toads and the like, really made a good meal off dirty plates on a vile table-cloth, our appetites being sharpened by the best of condiments.

Colonel Pickett has turned up here, having made his escape from Washington just in time to escape arrest—travelling in disguise on foot through out-of-the-way places till he got among friends.

I was glad, when bed-time approached, that I was not among the mattress men. One of the gentlemen in the bed next the door was a tremendous projector in the tobacco-juice line: his final rumination ere he sank to repose was a masterpiece of art—a perfect liquid pyrotechny, Roman candles and falling stars. A horrid thought occurred as I gazed and wondered. In case he should in a supreme moment turn his attention my way!—I was only seven or eight yards off, and that might be nothing to him!—I hauled down my musquito curtain at once, and watched him till, completely satiated, he slept.

May 5th.—Very warm, and no cold water, unless one went to the river. The hotel baths were not promising. This hotel is worse than Mill's House or Willard's. The feeding and the flies are intolerable. One of our party comes in to say that he could scarce get down to the hall on account of the crowd, and that all the people who passed him had very hard, sharp bones. He remarks thereupon to the clerk at the bar, who tells him that the particular projections he alludes to are implements of defence or offence, as the case may be, and adds, "I suppose you and your friends are the only people in the house who haven't a bowie-knife, or a six-shooter, or Derringer about them." The house is full of Confederate Congress men, politicians, colonels, and placemen with or without places, and a vast number of speculators, contractors, and the like, attracted by the embryo government. Among the visitors are many fillibusters, such as Henningsen, Pickett, Tochman, Wheat.* (Since killed in action.) I hear a good deal about the association called the Knights of the Golden Circle, a Protestant association for securing the Gulf provinces and states, including—which has been largely developed by recent events—them in the Southern Confederacy, and creating them into an independent government.

Montgomery has little claims to be called a capital. The streets are very hot, unpleasant, and uninteresting. I have rarely seen a more dull, lifeless place; it looks like a small Russian town in the interior. The names of the shopkeepers indicate German and French origin. I looked in at one or two of the slave magazines, which are not unlike similar establishments in Cairo and Smyrna. A certain degree of freedom is enjoyed by some of the men, who lounge about the doors, and are careless of escape or liberty, knowing too well the difficulties of either.

It is not in its external aspects generally that slavery is so painful. The observer must go with Sterne, and gaze in on the captives' dungeons through the bars. The condition of a pig in a stye is not, in an animal sense, anything but good. Well fed, over fed, covered from the winds and storms of heaven, with clothing, food, medicine provided, children taken care of, aged relatives and old age itself succoured and guarded—is not this—? Get thee behind us, slave philosopher! The hour comes when the butcher steals to the sty, and the knife leaps from the sheath.

Now there is this one thing in being an ἄναξ ἄνδρῶν that be the race of men bad as it may, a kind of grandiose character is given to their lender. The stag which sweeps his rivals from his course is the largest of the herd; but a man who drives the largest drove of sheep is no better than he who drives the smallest. The flock he compels must consist of human beings to develop the property of which I speak, and so the very superiority of the slave master in the ways and habits of command proves that the negro is a man. But, at the same time, the law which regulates all these relations between man and his fellows, asserts itself here. The dominant race becomes dependent on some other body of men, less martial, arrogant, and wealthy, for its elegances, luxuries, and necessaries. The poor villeins round the Norman castle forge the armour, make the furniture, and exercise the mechanical arts which the baron and his followers are too ignorant and too proud to pursue; if there is no population to serve this purpose, some energetic race comes in their place, and the Yankee does the part of the little hungry Greek to the Roman patrician.

The South has at present little or no manufactures, takes everything from the Yankee outside or the mean white within her gates, and despises both. Both are reconciled by interest. The one gets a good price for his manufacture and the fruit of his ingenuity from a careless, spendthrift proprietor; the other hopes to be as good as his master some day, and sees the beginning of his fortune in the possession of a negro. It is fortunate for our great British Catherine-wheel, which is continually throwing off light and heat to the remotest parts of the world—I hope not burning down to a dull red cinder in the centre at last—that it had not to send its emigrants to the Southern States, as assuredly the emigration would soon have been checked. The United States has been represented to the British and Irish emigrants by the free States—the Northern States and the great West—and the British and German emigrant who finds himself in the South, has drifted there through the Northern States, and either is a migratory labourer, or hopes to return with a little money to the North and West, if he does not see his way to the possession of land and negroes.

After dinner at the hotel table, which was crowded with officers, and where I met Mr. Howell Cobb and several senators of the new Congress, I spent the evening with Colonel Deas, Quartermaster-General, and a number of his staff, in their quarters. As I was walking over to the house, one of the detached villa-like residences so common in Southern cities, I perceived a crowd of very well-dressed negroes, men and women, in front of a plain brick building which I was informed was their Baptist meeting-house, into which white people rarely or never intrude. These were domestic servants, or persons employed in stores, and their general appearance indicated much comfort and even luxury. I doubted if they all were slaves. One of my companions went up to a young woman in a straw-hat, with bright red-and-green riband trimmings and artificial flowers, a gaudy Paisley shawl, and a rainbow-like gown, blown out over her yellow boots by a prodigious crinoline, and asked her "Whom do you belong to?" She replied, "I b'long to Massa Smith, sar." Well, we have men who "belong" to horses in England. I am not sure if Americans, North and South, do not consider their superiority to all Englishmen so thoroughly established, that they can speak of them as if they were talking of inferior animals. To-night, for example, a gallant young South Carolinian, one Ransome Calhoun,* (since killed) was good enough to say that "Great Britain was in mortal fear of France, and was abjectly subdued by her great rival." Hence came controversy, short and acrimonious.

May 6th.—I forgot to say that yesterday before dinner I drove out with some gentlemen and the ladies of the family of Mr. George N. Sanders, once United States' consul at Liverpool, now a doubtful man here, seeking some office from the Government, and accused by a portion of the press of being a Confederate spy—*Porcus de grege epicuri*—but a learned pig withal, and weather-wise, and mindful of the signs of the times, catching straws and whisking them upwards to detect the currents. Well, in this great moment I am bound to say there was much talk of ice. The North owns the frozen climates; but it was hoped that Great Britain, to whom belongs the North Pole, might force the blockade and send aid.

The environs of Montgomery are agreeable—well-wooded, undulating, villas abounding, public gardens, and a large negro and mulatto suburb. It is not usual, as far as I can judge, to see women riding on horseback in the South, but on the road here we encountered several.

After breakfast I walked down with Senator Wigfall to the capitol of Montgomery—one of the true Athenian Yankeeized structures of this novo-classic land, erected on a site worthy of a better fate and edifice. By an open cistern, on our way, I came on a gentleman engaged in disposing of some living ebony carvings to a small circle, who had more curiosity than cash, for they did not at all respond to the energetic appeals of the auctioneer.

The sight was a bad preparation for an introduction to the legislative assembly of a Confederacy which rests on the Institution as the cornerstone of the social and political arch which maintains it. But there they were, the legislators or conspirators, in a large room provided with benches and seats, and listening to such a sermon as a Balfour of Burley might have preached to his Covenanters—resolute and massive heads, and large frames—such men as must have a faith to inspire them. And that is so. Assaulted by reason, by logic, argument, philanthropy, progress directed against his peculiar institutions, the Southerner at last is driven to a fanaticism—a sacred faith which is above all reason or logical attack in the propriety, righteousness, and divinity of slavery.

The chaplain, a venerable old man, loudly invoked curses on the heads of the enemy, and blessings on the arms and councils of the New State. When he was done, Mr. Howell Cobb, a fat, double-chinned, mellow-eyed man, rapped with his hammer on the desk before the chair on which he sat as speaker of the assembly, and the house proceeded to business. I could fancy that, in all but garments, they were like the men who first conceived the great rebellion which led to the independence of this wonderful country—so earnest, so grave, so sober, and so vindictive—at least, so embittered against the power which they consider tyrannical and insulting.

The word "liberty" was used repeatedly in the short time allotted to the public transaction of business and the reading of documents; the Congress was anxious to get to its work, and Mr. Howell Cobb again thumped his desk and announced that the house was going into "secret session," which intimated that all persons who were not members should leave. I was introduced to what is called the floor of the house, and had a delegate's chair, and of course I moved away with the others, and with the disappointed ladies and men from the galleries, but one of the members, Mr. Rhett, I believe, said jokingly: "I think you ought to retain your seat. If the "Times" will support the South, we'll accept you as a delegate." I replied that I was afraid I could not act as a delegate to a Congress of Slave States. And, indeed, I had been much affected at the slave auction held just outside the hotel, on the steps of the public fountain, which I had witnessed on my way to the capitol. The auctioneer, who was an ill-favoured, dissipated-looking rascal, had his "article" beside him on, not in, a deal packing-case—a stout young negro badly dressed and ill-shod, who stood with all his goods fastened in a small bundle in his hand, looking out at the small and listless gathering of men, who, whittling and chewing, had moved out from the shady side of the street as they saw the man put up. The chattel character of slavery in the States renders it most repulsive. What a pity the nigger is not polypoid—so that he could be cut up in junks, and each junk should reproduce itself!

A man in a cart, some volunteers in coarse uniform, a few Irish labourers in a long van, and four or five men in the usual black coat, satin waistcoat, and black hat, constituted the audience, whom the auctioneer addressed volubly: "A prime field-hand! Just look at him—good-natered, well-tempered; no marks, nary sign of bad about him! En-i-ne hunthered—only nine hun-ther-ed and fifty dol'rs for 'em! Why, it's quite rad-aklous! Nine hundred and fifty dol'rs! I can't raly—That's good. Thank you, sir. Twenty-five bid—nine hun-therd and seventy-five dol'rs for this most useful hand." The price rose to one thousand dollars, at which the useful hand was knocked down to one of the black hats near me. The auctioneer and the negro and his buyer all walked off together to settle the transaction, and the crowd moved away.

"That nigger went cheap," said one of them to a companion, as he walked towards the shade. "Yes, *Sirr!* Niggers is cheap now—that's a fact." I must admit that I felt myself indulging in a sort of reflection whether it would not be nice to own a man as absolutely as one might possess a horse—to hold him subject to my will and pleasure, as if he were a brute beast without the power of kicking or biting—to make him work for me—to hold his fate in my hands: but the thought was for a moment. It was followed by disgust.

I have seen slave markets in the East, where the traditions of the race, the condition of family and social relations divest slavery of the most odious characteristics which pertain to it in the States; but the use of the English tongue in such transactions, and the idea of its taking place among a civilized Christian people, produced in me a feeling of inexpressible loathing and indignation. Yesterday I was much struck by the intelligence, activity, and desire to please of a good-looking coloured waiter, who seemed so light-hearted and light-coloured I could not imagine he was a slave. So one of our party, who was an American, asked him: "What are you, boy—a free nigger?" Of course he knew that in Alabama it was most unlikely he could reply in the affirmative. The young man's smile died away from his lips, a flush of blood embrowned the face for a moment, and he answered in a sad, low tone: "No, sir! I b'long to Massa Jackson," and left the room at once. As I stood at an upper window of the capitol, and looked on the wide expanse of richly-wooded, well-cultivated land which sweeps round the hill side away to the horizon, I could not help thinking of the misery and cruelty which must have been borne in tilling the land and raising the houses and streets of the dominant race before whom one nationality of coloured people have perished within the memory of man. The misery and cruelty of the system are established by the advertisements for runaway negroes, and by the description of the stigmata on their persons—whippings and brandings, scars and cuts—though these, indeed, are less frequent here than in the border States.

On my return, the Hon. W. M. Browne, Assistant Secretary of State, came to visit me—a cadet of an Irish family, who came to America some years ago, and having lost his money in land speculations, turned his pen to good account as a journalist, and gained Mr. Buchanan's patronage and support as a newspaper editor in Washington. There he became intimate with the Southern gentlemen, with whom he naturally associated in preference to the Northern members; and when they went out, he walked over along with them. He told me the Government had already received numerous—I think he said 400—letters from shipowners applying for letters of marque and reprisal. Many of these applications were from merchants in Boston, and other maritime cities in the New England States. He further stated that the President was determined to take the whole control of the army, and the appointments to command in all ranks of officers into his own hands.

There is now no possible chance of preserving the peace or of averting the horrors of war from these great and prosperous communities. The Southern people, right or wrong, are bent on independence and on separation, and they will fight to the last for their object.

The press is fanning the flame on both sides: it would be difficult to say whether it or the telegraphs circulate lies most largely; but that as the papers print the telegrams, they must have the palm. The Southerners are told there is a reign of terror in New York—that the 7th New York

Regiment has been captured by the Baltimore people—that Abe Lincoln is always drunk—that General Lee has seized Arlington heights, and is bombarding Washington. The New York people are regaled with similar stories from the South. The coincidence between the date of the skirmish at Lexington and of the attack on the 6th Massachusetts Regiment at Baltimore is not so remarkable as the fact, that the first man who was killed at the latter place, 86 years ago, was a direct descendant of the first of the colonists who was killed by the royal soldiery. Baltimore may do the same for the South which Lexington did for all the Colonies. Head-shaving, forcible deportations, tarring and feathering are recommended and adopted as specifics to produce conversion from erroneous opinions. The President of the United States has called into service of the Federal Government 42,000 volunteers, and increased the regular army by 22,000 men, and the navy by 18,000 men. If the South secede, they ought certainly to take over with them some Yankee hotel keepers. This "Exchange" is in a frightful state—nothing but noise, dirt, drinking, wrangling.

CHAPTER XXIII.

. . . *May 9th.*—To-day the papers contain a proclamation by the President of the Confederate States of America, declaring a state of war between the Confederacy and the United States, and notifying the issue of letters of marque and reprisal. I went out with Mr. Wigfall in the forenoon to pay my respects to Mr. Jefferson Davis at the State Department. Mr. Seward told me that but for Jefferson Davis the Secession plot could never have been carried out. No other man of the party had the brain, or the courage and dexterity, to bring it to a successful issue. All the persons in the Southern States spoke of him with admiration, though their forms of speech and thought generally forbid them to be respectful to any one.

There before me was "Jeff Davis's State Department"—a large brick building, at the corner of a street, with a Confederate flag floating above it. The door stood open, and "gave" on a large hall white-washed, with doors plainly painted belonging to small rooms, in which was transacted most important business, judging by the names written on sheets of paper and applied outside, denoting bureaux of the highest functions. A few clerks were passing in and out, and one or two gentlemen were on the stairs, but there was no appearance of any bustle in the building.

We walked straight up-stairs to the first-floor, which was surrounded by doors opening from a quadrangular platform. On one of these was written simply, "The President." Mr. Wigfall went in, and after a moment returned and said, "The President will be glad to see you; walk in, sir." When I entered, the President was engaged with four gentlemen, who were making some offer of aid to him. He was thanking them "in the name of the Government." Shaking hands with each, he saw them to the door, bowed them and Mr. Wigfall out, and turning to me said, "Mr. Russell, I am glad to welcome you here, though I fear your appearance is a symptom that our affairs are not quite prosperous," or words to that effect. He then requested me to sit down close to his own chair at his office-table, and proceeded to speak on general matters, adverting to the Crimean War and the Indian Mutiny, and asking questions about Sebastopol, the Redan, and the Siege of Lucknow.

I had an opportunity of observing the President very closely: he did not impress me as favourably as I had expected, though he is certainly a very different looking man from Mr. Lincoln. He is like a gentleman—has a slight, light figure, little exceeding middle height, and holds himself erect and straight. He was dressed in a rustic suit of slate-coloured stuff, with a black silk handkerchief round his neck; his manner is plain, and rather reserved and drastic; his head is well formed, with a fine full forehead, square and high, covered with innumerable fine lines and wrinkles, features regular, though the check-bones are too high, and the jaws too hollow to be handsome; the lips are thin, flexible, and curved, the chin square, well-defined; the nose very regular, with wide nostrils; and the eyes deep set, large and full—one seems nearly blind, and is partly covered with a film, owing to excruciating attacks of neuralgia and tic. Wonderful to relate, he does not chew, and is neat and clean-looking, with hair trimmed and boots brushed. The expression of his face is anxious, he has a very haggard, care-worn, and pain-drawn look, though no trace of anything but the utmost confidence and the greatest decision could be detected in his conversation. He asked me some questions respecting the route I had taken in the States.

I mentioned that I had seen great military preparations through the South, and was astonished at the alacrity with which the people sprang to arms. "Yes, sir," he remarked, and his tone of voice and manner of speech are rather remarkable for what are considered Yankee peculiarities, "in Europe" (Mr. Seward also indulges in that pronunciation) "they laugh at us because of our fondness for military titles and displays. All your travellers in this country have commented on the number of generals, and colonels, and majors all over the States. But the fact is, we are a military people, and these signs of the fact were ignored. We are not less military because we have had no great standing armies. But perhaps we are the only people in the world where gentlemen go to a military academy, who do not intend to follow the profession of arms."

In the course of our conversation, I asked him to have the goodness to direct that a sort of passport or protection should be given to me, as I might possibly fall in with some guerilla leader on my way northwards, in whose eyes I might not be entitled to safe conduct. Mr. Davis said, "I shall give such instructions to the Secretary of War as shall be necessary. But, sir, you are among civilized, intelligent people who understand your position, and appreciate your character. We do not seek the sympathy of England by unworthy means, for we respect ourselves, and we are glad to invite the scrutiny of men into our acts; as for our motives, we meet the eye of Heaven." I thought I could judge from his words that he had the highest idea of the French as soldiers, but that his feelings and associations were more identified with England, although he was quite aware of the difficulty of conquering the repugnance which exists to slavery.

Mr. Davis made no allusion to the authorities at Washington, but he asked me if I thought it was supposed in England there would be war between the two States? I answered, that I was under the impression the public thought there would be no actual hostilities. "And yet you see we are driven to take up arms for the defence of our rights and liberties."

As I saw an immense mass of papers on his table, I rose and made my bow, and Mr. Davis, seeing me to the door, gave me his hand and said, "As long as you may stay among us you shall receive every facility it is in our power to afford to you, and I shall always be glad to see you." Colonel

"Drumming Up Recruits for the Confederate Army," in front of Montgomery's Exchange Hotel, from Harper's Weekly, *1 June 1861.*

Wigfall was outside, and took me to the room of the Secretary of War, Mr. Walker, whom we found closeted with General Beauregard and two other officers in a room full of maps and plans. He is the kind of man generally represented in our types of a "Yankee"— tall, lean, straight-haired, angular, with fiery, impulsive eyes and manner—a ruminator of tobacco and a profuse spitter—a lawyer, I believe, certainly not a soldier; ardent, devoted to the cause, and confident to the last degree of its speedy success.

The news that two more States had joined the Confederacy, making ten in all, was enough to put them in good humour. "Is it not too bad these Yankees will not let us go our own way, and keep their cursed Union to themselves? If they force us to it, we may be obliged to drive them beyond the Susquehanna." Beauregard was in excellent spirits, busy measuring off miles of country with his compass, as if he were dividing empires.

From this room I proceeded to the office of Mr. Benjamin, the Attorney-General of the Confederate States, the most brilliant perhaps of the whole of the famous Southern orators. He is a short, stout man, with a full face, olive-coloured, and most decidedly Jewish features, with the brightest large black eyes, one of which is somewhat diverse from the other, and a brisk, lively, agreeable manner, combined with much vivacity of speech and quickness of utterance. He is one of the first lawyers or advocates in the United States, and had a large practice at Washington, where his annual receipts from his profession were not less than £8000 to £10,000 a year. But his love of the card-table rendered him a prey to older and cooler hands, who waited till the sponge was full at the end of the session, and then squeezed it to the last drop.

Mr. Benjamin is the most open, frank, and cordial of the Confederates whom I have yet met. In a few seconds he was telling me all about the course of Government with respect to privateers and letters of marque and reprisal, in order probably to ascertain what were our views in England on the subject. I observed it was likely the North would not respect their flag, and would treat their privateers as pirates. "We have an easy remedy for that. For any man under our flag whom the authorities of the United States dare to execute, we shall hang two of their people." "Suppose, Mr. Attorney-General, England, or any of the great powers which decreed the abolition of privateering, refuses to recognise your flag?" "We intend to claim, and do claim, the exercise of all the rights and privileges of an independent sovereign State, and any attempt to refuse us the full measure of those rights would be an act of hostility to our country." "But if England, for example, declared your privateers were pirates?" "As the United States never admitted the principle laid down at the Congress of Paris, neither have the Confederate States. If England thinks fit to declare privateers under our flag pirates, it would be nothing more or less than a declaration of war against us, and we must meet it as best we can." In fact, Mr. Benjamin did not appear afraid of anything; but his confidence respecting Great Britain was based a good deal, no doubt, on his firm faith in cotton, and in England's utter subjection to her cotton interest and manufactures. "All this coyness about acknowledging a slave power will come right at last. We hear our commissioners have gone on to Paris, which looks as if they had met with no encouragement at London; but we are quite easy in our minds on this point at present."

So Great Britain is in a pleasant condition, Mr. Seward is threatening us with war if we recognise the South, and the South declares that if we don't recognise their flag, they will take it as an act of hostility. Lord Lyons is pressed to give an assurance to the Government at Washington, that under no circumstances will Great Britain recognise the Southern rebels; but, at the same time, Mr. Seward refuses to give any assurance whatever that the right of neutrals will be respected in the impending struggle.

As I was going down stairs, Mr. Browne called me into his room. He said that the Attorney-General and himself were in a state of perplexity as to the form in which letters of marque and reprisal should be made out. They had consulted all the books they could get, but found no examples to suit their case, and he wished to know, as I was a barrister, whether I could aid him. I told him it was not so much my regard to my own position as a neutral, as the *vafri inscitia juris* which prevented me throwing any light on the subject. There are not only Yankee shipowners but English firms ready with sailors and steamers for the Confederate Government, and the owner of the Camilla might be tempted to part with his yacht by the offers made to him.

Being invited to attend a levée or reception held by Mrs. Davis, the President's wife, I returned to the hotel to prepare for the occasion. On my way I passed a company of volunteers, one hundred and twenty artillerymen, and three field-pieces, on their way to the station for Virginia, followed by a crowd of "citizens" and negroes of both sexes, cheering vociferously. The band was playing that excellent quick-step "Dixie." The men were stout, fine fellows, dressed in coarse grey tunics with yellow facings, and French caps. They were armed with smooth-bore muskets, and their knapsacks were unfit for marching, being water-proof bags slung from the shoulders. The guns had no caissons, and the shoeing of the troops was certainly deficient in soleing. The Zouave mania is quite as rampant here as it is in New York, and the smallest children are thrust into baggy red breeches, which the learned Lipsius might have appreciated, and are sent out with flags and tin swords to impede the highways.

The modest villa in which the President lives is painted white—another "White House"—and stands in a small garden. The door was open. A coloured servant took in our names, and Mr. Browne presented me to Mrs. Davis, whom I could just make out in the *demi-jour* of a moderately-sized parlour, surrounded by a few ladies and gentlemen, the former in bonnets, the latter in morning dress *à la midi*. There was no affectation of state or

"The White House at Montgomery—Rent $5,000 a year," from Harper's Weekly, *1 June 1861.*

ceremony in the reception. Mrs. Davis, whom some of her friends call "Queen Varina," is a comely, sprightly woman, verging on matronhood, of good figure and manners, well-dressed, lady-like, and clever, and she seemed a great favourite with those around her, though I did hear one of them say "It must be very nice to be the President's wife, and be the first lady in the Confederate States." Mrs. Davis, whom the President C. S. married *en secondes noces,* exercised considerable social influence in Washington, where I met many of her friends. She was just now inclined to be angry, because the papers contained a report that a reward was offered in the North for the head of the arch rebel Jeff Davis. "They are quite capable, I believe," she said, "of such acts." There were not more than eighteen or twenty persons present, as each party came in and staid only for a few moments, and, after a time, I made my bow and retired, receiving from Mrs. Davis an invitation to come in the evening, when I would find the President at home.

At sundown, amid great cheering, the guns in front of the State Department fired ten rounds, to announce that Tennessee and Arkansas had joined the Confederacy.

In the evening I dined with Mr. Benjamin and his brother-in-law, a gentleman of New Orleans, Colonel Wigfall coming in at the end of dinner. The New Orleans people of French descent, or "Creoles," as they call themselves, speak French in preference to English, and Mr. Benjamin's brother-in-law laboured considerably in trying to make himself understood in our vernacular. The conversation, Franco-English, very pleasant, for Mr. Benjamin is agreeable and lively. He is certain that the English law authorities must advise the Government that the blockade of the Southern ports is illegal so long as the President claims them to be ports of the United States. "At present," he said, "their paper blockade does no harm; the season for shipping cotton is over; but in October next, when the Mississippi is floating cotton by the thousands of bales, and all our wharves are full, it is inevitable that the Yankees must come to trouble with this attempt to coerce us." Mr. Benjamin walked back to the hotel with me, and we found our room full of tobacco-smoke, filibusters, and conversation, in which, as sleep was impossible, we were obliged to join.

I resisted a vigorous attempt of Mr. G. N. Sanders and a friend of his to take me to visit a planter who had a beaver-dam some miles outside Montgomery. They succeeded in capturing Mr. Deasy.

CHAPTER XXIV.

. . . *May 8th.*—I tried to write, as I have taken my place in the steamer to Mobile to-morrow, and I was obliged to do my best in a room full of people, constantly disturbed by visitors. Early this morning, as usual, my faithful Wigfall comes in and sits by my bedside, and passing his hands through his locks, pours out his ideas with wonderful lucidity and odd affectation of logic all his own. "We are a peculiar people, sir! You don't understand us, and you can't understand us, because we are known to you only by Northern writers and Northern papers, who know nothing of us themselves, or misrepresent what they do know. We are an agricultural people; we are a primitive but a civilized people. We have no cities—we don't want them. We have no literature—we don't need any yet. We have no press—we are glad of it. We do not require a press, because we go out and discuss all public questions from the stump with our people. We have no commercial marine—no navy—we don't want them. We are better without them. Your ships carry our produce, and you can protect your own vessels. We want no manufactures: we desire no trading, no mechanical or manufacturing classes. As long as we have our rice, our sugar, our tobacco, and our cotton, we can command wealth to purchase all we want from those nations with which we are in amity, and to lay up money besides. But with the Yankees we will never trade—never. Not one pound of cotton shall ever go from the South to their accursed cities; not one ounce of their steel or their manufactures shall ever cross our border." And so on. What the Senator who is preparing a bill for drafting the people into the army fears is, that the North will begin active operations before the South is ready for resistance. "Give us till November to drill our men, and we shall be irresistible." He deprecates any offensive movement, and is opposed to an attack on Washington, which many journals here advocate.

Mr. Walker sent me over a letter recommending me to all officers of the Confederate States, and I received an invitation from the President to dine with him to-morrow, which I was much chagrined to be obliged to refuse. In fact, it is most important to complete my Southern tour speedily, as all mail communication will soon be suspended from the South, and the blockade effectually cuts off any communication by sea. Rails torn up, bridges broken, telegraphs down—trains searched—the war is begun. The North is pouring its hosts to the battle, and it has met the paeans of the conquering Charlestonians with a universal yell of indignation and an oath of vengeance.

I expressed a belief in a letter, written a few days after my arrival (March 27th), that the South would never go back into the Union. The North think that they can coerce the South, and I am not prepared to say they are right or wrong; but I am convinced that the South can only be forced back by such a conquest as that which laid Poland prostrate at the feet of Russia. It may be that such a conquest can be made by the North, but success must destroy the Union as it has been constituted in times past. A strong Government must be the logical consequence of victory, and the triumph of the South will be attended by a similar result, for which, indeed, many Southerners are very well disposed. To the people of the Confederate States there would be no terror in such an issue, for it appears to me they are pining for a strong Government exceedingly. The North must accept it, whether they like it or not.

Neither party—if such a term can be applied to the rest of the United States, and to those States which disclaim the authority of the Federal Government—was prepared for the aggressive or resisting power of the other. Already the Confederate States perceive that they cannot carry all before them with a rush, while the North have learnt that they must put forth all their strength to make good a tithe of their lately uttered threats. But the Montgomery Government are anxious to gain time, and to prepare a regular army. The North, distracted by apprehensions of vast disturbance in their complicated relations, are clamouring for instant action and speedy consummation. The counsels of moderate men, as they were called, have been utterly overruled.

The whole foundation on which South Carolina rests is cotton and a certain amount of rice; or rather she bases her whole fabric on the necessity which exists in Europe for those products of her soil, believing and asserting, as she does, that England and France cannot and will not do without them. Cotton, without a market, is so much flocculent matter encumbering the ground. Rice, without demand for it, is unsaleable grain in store and on the field. Cotton at ten cents a pound is boundless prosperity, empire and superiority, and rice or grain need no longer be regarded.

In the matter of slave-labour, South Carolina argues pretty much in the following manner: England and France (she says) require our products. In order to meet their wants, we must cultivate our soil. There is only one way of doing so. The white man cannot live on our land at certain seasons of the year; he cannot work in the manner required by the crops. He must, therefore, employ a race suited to the labour, and that is a race which will only work when it is obliged to do so. That race was imported from Africa, under the sanction of the law, by our ancestors, when we were a British colony, and it has been fostered by us, so that its increase here has been as great as that of the most flourishing people in the world. In other places, where its labour was not productive or imperatively essential, that race has been made free, sometimes with disastrous consequences to itself and to industry. But we will not make it free. We cannot do so. We hold that slavery is essential to our existence as producers of what Europe requires; nay more, we maintain it is in the abstract right in principle, and some of us go so far as to maintain that the only proper form of society, according to the law of God and the exigencies of man, is that which has slavery as its basis. As to the slave, he is happier far in his state of servitude, more civilised and religious, than he is or could be if free or in his native Africa. For this system we will fight to the end.

In the evening I paid farewell visits, and spent an hour with Mr. Toombs, who is unquestionably one of the most original, quaint, and earnest of the Southern leaders, and whose eloquence and power as a debater are greatly esteemed by his countrymen. He is something of an Anglo-maniac, and an Anglo-phobist—a combination not unusual in America—that is, he is proud of being connected with and descended from respectable English families, and admires our mixed constitution, whilst he is an enemy to what is called English policy, and is a strong pro-slavery champion. Wigfall and he are very uneasy about the scant supply of gunpowder in the Southern States, and the difficulty of obtaining it.

In the evening had a little reunion in the bedroom as before—Mr. Wigfall, Mr. Keitt, an eminent Southern politician, Colonel Pickett, Mr. Browne, Mr. Benjamin, Mr. George Sanders, and others. The last-named gentleman was dismissed or recalled from his post at Liverpool, because he fraternised with Mazzini and other Red Republicans *à ce qu' on dit.* Here he is a slavery man, and a friend of an oligarchy. Your "Rights of Man" man is often most inconsistent with himself, and is generally found associated with the men of force and violence.

May the 9th.—My faithful Wigfall was good enough to come in early, in order to show me some comments on my letters in the "New York Times." It appears the papers are angry because I said that New York was apathetic when I landed, and they try to prove I was wrong by showing there was a "glorious outburst of Union feeling," after the news of the fall of Sumter. But I now know that the very apathy of which I spoke was felt by the Government of Washington, and was most weakening and embarrassing to them. What would not the value of "the glorious outburst" have been, had it taken place *before* the Charleston batteries had opened on Sumter — when the Federal flag, for example, was fired on, flying from the 'Star of the West,' or when Beauregard cut off supplies, or Bragg threatened Pickens, or the first shovel of earth was thrown up in hostile battery? But no! New York was then engaged in discussing State rights, and in reading articles to prove the new Government would be traitors if they endeavoured to reinforce the Federal forts, or were perusing leaders in favor of the Southern Government. Haply, they may remember one, not so many weeks old, in which the "New York Herald" compared Jeff Davis and his Cabinet to the "Great Rail Splitter," and Seward, and Chase, and came to the conclusion that the former "were gentlemen"—(a matter of which it is quite incompetent to judge)—"and would, and ought to succeed." The glorious outburst of "Union feeling" which threatened to demolish the "Herald" office, has created a most wonderful change in the views of the proprietor, whose diverse-eyed vision is now directed solely to the beauties of the Union, and whose faith is expressed in "a hearty adhesion to the Government of our country." New York must pay the penalty of its indifference, and bear the consequences of listening to such counsellors.

Mr. Deasy, much dilapidated, returned about twelve o'clock from his planter, who was drunk when he went over, and would not let him go to the beaver-dam. To console him, the planter stayed up all night drinking, and waking him up at intervals, that he might refresh him with a glass of whisky. This man was well off, owned land, and a good stock of slaves, but he must have been a "mean white," who had raised himself in the world. He lived in a three-roomed wooden cabin, and in one of the rooms he kept his wife shut up from the strangers' gaze. One of his negroes was unwell, and he took Deasy to see him. The result of his examination was, "Nigger! I guess you won't live more than an hour." His diagnosis was quite correct.

Before my departure I had a little farewell levée—Mr. Toombs, Mr. Browne, Mr. Benjamin, Mr. Walker, Major Deas, Colonel Pickett, Major Calhoun, Captain Ripley, and others—who were exceedingly kind with letters of introduction and offers of service. Dined as usual on a composite dinner—Southern meat and poultry bad—at three o'clock, and at four P.M. drove down to the steep banks of the Alabama River, where the castle-like hulk of the "Southern Republic" was waiting to receive us. I bade good-by to Montgomery without regret. The native people were not very attractive, and the city has nothing to make up for their deficiency, but of my friends there I must always retain pleasant memories, and, indeed, I hope some day I shall be able to keep my promise to return and see more of the Confederate ministers and their chief.

Index

D

Donal McIlraith has made a unique contribution to the interpretation of the most challenging book in the New Testament. There is no single answer to the "meaning" of any text. This is especially true of the elusive Book of Revelation. There are *many* interpretations possible, but this does not mean that *any* interpretation is good enough. Starting with the rich nuptial imagery of the closing chapters of Revelation, Dr. McIlraith uses the overt use of the theme of love and intimacy *found in the text* as a key for the interpretation of the whole book. The results of his work break open this treasure from Christian Tradition, relating it to the lived experience of all who hope to follow the Lamb.

FRANCIS J. MOLONEY, SDB, Senior Professorial Fellow, Catholic Theological College, University of Divinity, Melbourne

Everyone's Apocalypse is a thoughtful study of Revelation that is accessible to all readers. Father McIlraith emphasizes the love story that undergirds the whole book: Christ the Bridegroom and his Bride, the Church. Prophetic symbols and natural disasters abound, but it all turns on Christ's triumph and justice that call forth our love, faith, service, and endurance. The format helps the reader to slow down and ponder, with reflection questions and prayer suggestions after each section. I will heartily recommend it to both friends and students.

KATHRYN WEHR, Managing Editor, *Logos: A Journal of Catholic Thought and Culture*, University of St. Thomas, St. Paul, Minnesota

This exposition of the Book of Revelation is worth its weight in gold, and so much more. Father McIlraith's expansive missionary experience and scholarly expertise shine through every page of his reflections on the nuptial love of Jesus, the apocalyptic Lamb, for his people in the Church. And only someone deeply enamored himself with the bride of Christ could have written such a readable guide to one of the most thought-provoking books of Sacred Scripture. With at the same time contemplative and pastoral intuitiveness, the author urges us to share in Jesus' victory through the trials of the present life. He almost effortlessly, but also amiably, unriddles even the most bewildering symbols of the biblical text, leading the reader into prayerful pondering of their spiritual meaning. If you are looking for an eminently perspicacious and reliable pathfinder into this world of redemptive message, *Everyone's Apocalypse* is the book for you.

ANDREAS HOECK, author of *Worthy Lamb: An Exegetical-Spiritual Commentary on John's Apocalypse*, and professor and chair of Sacred Scripture, Saint John Vianney Theological Seminary, Denver, Colorado